AF484673

OH MOTHER, WHAT HAVE YOU DONE?

THE MAKING OF PSYCHO II

**TOM HOLLAND
RICHARD FRANKLIN
& ANDREW LONDON**

WITH AFTERWORD BY ANTHONY S. CIPRIANO

Copyright © 2023 by Holland House. All rights reserved.

Photographs and production materials from the personal collections of Tom Holland and Richard Franklin, with contributions by Richard Franklin excerpted from his memoir (published with kind permission from Jennifer Hadden.)

No part of this book may be reproduced in any form or by any electronic or mechanical means, including information storage and retrieval systems, without written permission from the author, except for the use of brief quotations in a book review.

Table of Contents

Introduction
by Tom Holland

Reading Richard's memoirs for the first time was like stepping back 40 years. I am writing this on the anniversary of *Psycho II* on June 10, 2023. The movie itself opened June 3, 1983. Is that possible? It doesn't seem like yesterday, but it sure doesn't feel that long ago either.

Richard Franklin and I went through a lot and then lost touch as careers will do and got together down the line and during the in-betweens here in LA when he and his lovely wife, Jennifer Hadden, would come through. We discussed much of what he wrote below about *Psycho II*, but I've never experienced a filmmaker's memories of his creative work on a project, especially a sequel to a worldwide famous horror movie.

Richard takes us all the way from getting the job, to conceiving the film, to hiring me as the writer, getting it shot and edited and released, and watching the results. His memories left me open-mouthed.

I was there for all of it but reliving the director's experience from the point of view of the writer brought so many moments back to me.

To make it even more piquant, Richard did this after he had returned Down Under to stay and time was growing short, and I didn't know about it. It was only when the Aussie documentary maker, Mark Hartley, came by with 4K's of *Cloak & Dagger*, the film that Richard and I did after *Psycho II*, that I found out about his memoirs, and read them.

Richard had cancer, the same disease that had taken his father just a few years before the two of us began work on *Psycho II*. The experience of working on that film with Richard changed me as a writer and human being. As I read Richard's words, I realized how important the experience was for both of us, but especially me, and I wanted to remember how the fusion of so many talented people came together to make what was an exceptional sequel, that launched a legacy that lives to this day.

All because of the genius of Alfred Hitchcock.

Screenwriter Tom Holland with director Richard Franklin

Chapter 1
Before The Beginning

Richard Franklin: My first inkling that a sequel to *Psycho* was in the wind had come in August 1981, when Robert Bloch and I were speakers at a Sci-Fi convention in Melbourne. Bloch told me he was writing the book, and the audacity of his idea of picking up the story twenty years later (instead of the usual few weeks) hit me like Norman's shovel. It was an exciting raison d'etre for any sequel, but the idea of finding out what had happened to one of the screen's archetypes, twenty years on was irresistible (like *Casablanca II - What Happened to Rick and Ilsa?* or JM Barrie's suppressed *When Wendy Grew Up*).

Tom Holland: Read below because you're seeing Richard putting together the pieces to make a brilliant jump-off Robert Bloch's *Psycho II* novel that everybody hated. So, he knows Psycho II is going to deal with Norman Bates 22 years later.

Richard Franklin: At the time, I had phoned and asked my agent to speak to Bloch's publishers, but found out that although Bloch could publish a book, the rights to a *Psycho* movie sequel were automatically Universal's. I, therefore, gave it no more thought, until a phone call that October from my *Roadgames* Executive Producer Bernard Schwartz.

Andrew London: I introduced Richard to Bernie in 1979 when he and his co-producer, Barbi Taylor, came to Los Angeles to get the ball rolling on *Roadgames*. At the time, I was supervising the sound mix on *Coal Miner's Daughter* at Robert Altman's Lionsgate Films, and I told them to meet me for lunch, and I would introduce them to our producer, Bernard Schwartz.

Bernie later brought Richard to meet Bob Rehme at Avco Embassy, which later went on to finance and distribute *Roadgames* internationally.

Richard told me that, sometime later, they bumped into Janet Leigh. Upon being introduced to Bernie, she said, rather tongue-in-cheek: "Wasn't I married to you at one time?" (Her ex-husband Tony Curtis was born Bernard Schwartz). Later on, when Richard wanted to hire me to edit *Psycho II*, Bernie promised me that, were I not hired as editor (Universal had Richard see many of their top editors at the time), he wanted me to do the sound editing for the film.

The gossip going around Universal once I was hired as editor was: "Have you heard, a sound editor is doing the film editing?" Later, when I held Bernie to his promise, the gossip became: "Have you heard the film editor is doing the sound?"

Richard Franklin: He told me Universal was thinking of doing a sequel to *Psycho* - what did I think? I told him of my meeting with Bloch and waxed lyrical. He said he'd get back to me when the galleys of the book were available.

A few weeks later, he called back. Universal had dropped the idea because the book was lousy. He began to read me a synopsis: "Norman strangles a nun with her rosary beads, then escapes from prison in drag..." He didn't have to go any further. I interrupted him. "Hitchcock's Norman would never kill a nun. And in any case, he would not have gone to prison, but to a psychiatric hospital where he would have been a model inmate, tending the flowers. So, with the insanity plea, he wouldn't need to escape, as they would be letting him go... about now."

Tom Holland: This is what Richard gave me to work with as the screenwriter, a vision of the *Psycho* house and the motel below, with the stone stairway up, and a great story premise: "It's 22 years later – and Norman is coming home."

The huge overwhelming downer was that Tony Perkins did not want to do it – but would glance at a script – *Psycho II* was to be a cable movie. Cable networks to distribute info and entertainment were just then being built across the country. At the time, that wasn't even as certain as a TV movie to be produced.

Therefore, we were originally a direct-to-cable movie for a new cable company in San Diego. You'll see it in the opening credits. Oak Industries is one of the producers.

If we wanted to get the movie made and have a theatrical release, both Richard and I realized we needed Tony Perkins to play Norman Bates. But how to get him to say "yes?" I knew I had to tell a story that any actor would love and could not turn down. Having started out as an actor (and having spent what seemed like most of my life up to that point in "scene study" classes) I had a good idea of what made an actor fall in love with a part. After all, among my teachers had been Lee Strasberg, Stella Adler, and Sandy Meisner, each of whom taught a different method, but they all agreed on one thing: find the character arc.

How about being released from the insane asylum, *and returning* to the site of the horror 22 years later, only to find someone is trying to drive you insane again?

Hmmm, interesting idea.

Franklin and Holland (as Deputy Norris) discussing the scene

Chapter 2
The Sequel That Shouldn't Be Made

Richard Franklin: The first Universal executive I met was Hilton Green. The son of director Alfred E Green (*The Jolson Story*), he had been Universal's head of production and according to Bernie, the Universal hierarchy was giving him *Psycho II* as a "golden handshake" from his position in the tower.

Hilton had been the assistant director on *Psycho* and the Hitchcock television show, and I believe his involvement was the main reason the production seemed blessed from the outset. Not only is he one of the best line producers (and nicest men) I've ever worked with, but because he was still a Vice President of the company, Universal did not follow their usual practice of assigning an executive "watchdog" to the production. Thus *Psycho II* was made without interference from the so-called "front office," and it was bliss.

Andrew London: Richard and I first met in 1967 as students at the film school of USC, where we organized one of the earliest retrospectives of the film and TV work of Alfred Hitchcock. We bonded over our mutual love of *Vertigo* – virtually analyzing it frame-by-frame on a stop-and-go projector. Richard brought Hitch to speak to the students, and later was invited by Hitch to observe some of the filming of *Topaz*. It is no wonder that the thriller genre became Richard's most comfortable arena in which to work.

1968 - Richard Franklin and Alfred Hitchcock at USC (University of Southern California) for a Hitchcock retrospective.

Chapter 3
Getting The Deal

Richard Franklin: There were a couple of weeks of uncertainty while my deal was struck, but even though my agent was dubious, it never crossed my mind *Psycho II* would not happen. I was so high, my favorite song at the time was 'Rich and Happy' from Sondheim's *Merrily We Roll Along* (Steve meant the song ironically but for a few months, it was my anthem) I was not rich, but I was certainly happy.

Andrew London: I initiated Richard into the world of Sondheim in 1974 when he invited me to Australia to edit his first film *The True Story of Eskimo Nell*. Having recently seen *A Little Night Music* on Broadway, I gifted him with the original cast recording, setting up a devoted fandom that rivaled his one for Hitchcock, and that culminated in their correspondence that ended only with Richard's untimely passing in 2007.

Richard Franklin: The deal at Universal was still only for the "development" of a screenplay, and had I known about the difficulty of getting the so-called "green light", I might have been less enthusiastic. But I suspect it was my enthusiasm and ignorance of Hollywood ("confidence of ignorance," as Orson Welles called it) which kept the whole thing afloat.

At the same time, I was introduced to Hilton Green, our line producer, if the deal went through. He quizzed me about Hitchcock and *Psycho*, but it was not long before he was generously telling people that he'd worked with Hitchcock for twenty-five years, but I knew more about the man and his movies.

Tom Holland: Hilton Green was all those things and had been Mr. Hitchcock's First AD on *Psycho* as well as others. He put together a crew on *Psycho II* which was the last stand of those who had actually worked with the Master. It was incredible. I went around, talking to them all about what working with Mr. Hitchcock was like. There wasn't a lot of personal warmth, but there was a huge amount of respect.

Richard Franklin: At one point Tony Perkins' agent told us he would definitely not do a *Psycho* sequel and I persuaded Bernie to keep going on the assumption they were bluffing.

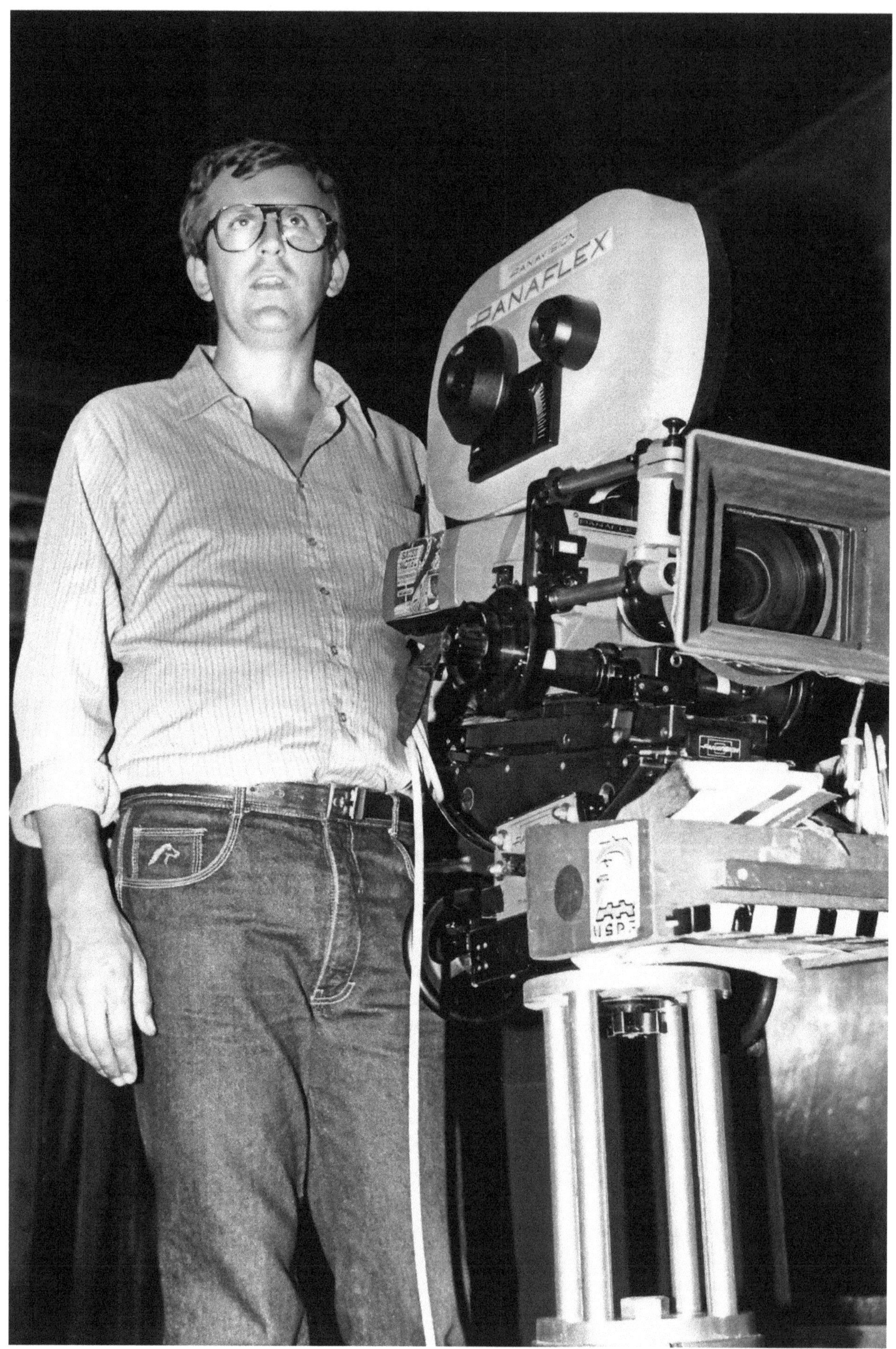

PANAVISION
PANAFLEX
USP

Director Richard Franklin setting up a shot with director of photography Dean Cundey (far right)

Chapter 4
The Challenge

Richard Franklin: I later discovered not only was Tony angling to direct the picture, but that former Hitchcock associate Norman Lloyd (the namesake of *Saboteur*) had also been proposed by Hilton as the man to direct.

Tom Holland: Reading this is a bit of a surprise after all these years. I knew about Norman Lloyd, but not that Tony wanted to direct. Richard never told me, hmmm. However, it makes sense. Tony ended up directing *Psycho III*.

I thought it was because Universal had not paid his deferment, based on gross, which was enormous for the time – The latter not the former – He threatened to sue. Told me the exec said he'd never work in town again if he did that. Tony said, "Sure, until you need me again."

He got his money and triggered my much smaller deferment. "Thank you, Tony."

It's also why Tony demanded that he direct *Psycho III*. Without Norman (Bates, not Lloyd), you didn't have a *Psycho* movie, especially not after *II*.

Richard Franklin: But I was unstoppable. And best of all, the creative juices were flowing. I awakened Denise (my then wife) at five one morning to describe a scene which was the seed from which the whole story grew. I literally had a "vision" - of Norman staring up the staircase as someone dressed as his mother came down towards him.

Tom Holland: Yes, this was another stroke of visual genius that Richard brought with him, one of many. He had certain shots in his head, a whole collection of them, he'd thought about it for so long. The Psycho House, as it is now called, with the motel from hell below (with Dennis Franz as the clerk, no less) was to be the heart of the movie. And it was 22 years later, and Norman Bates was coming home. That was a Hell of a premise to base a sequel on.

Richard Franklin: It was the audience seeing the scene from two perspectives, objectively and from the character's point of view. I kept the idea to myself while I waited for my deal to "close" and at last my agent told me I had an office at Universal Studios.

Everyone to whom I talked as I embarked on the project, told me the same thing: the task of sequelizing *Psycho*, of re-creating a screen legend, was unassailable. That even if I made *Citizen Kane* the picture would be reviled, and my career ended in one fell swoop –

Tom Holland: Everybody told me the same thing: my writing career would be finished if I wrote a sequel to *Psycho*. But my career wasn't in that good shape to begin with. I had spent most of my thirties writing spec scripts and finally got my first one produced, *The Beast Within*, only to have it be the last film United Artists released as the company was buried in the wreckage of *Heaven's Gate*.

It made $, too, not the Cimino film, but *The Beast Within*, only no one knew, and I had spent almost a year unemployed before Richard offered me *Psycho II*. So, you see, I didn't have much to lose, and who knew what to gain, but, like Richard, *Psycho* had been a seminal moment in my absolute love of film and an experience that I did not forget.

I was 14 or 15 and spent my time slumped low in my seat, watching the movie through my fingers I was so terrified. I don't think I really understood what editing was until that moment. The shower scene was so overwhelming that I became aware that it was put together from different angles, different shots. I only dimly understood that at the time.

Now at 38 I was going to do a deep dive into Hitch's magic – and how Richard used and recreated it and made it his own. At the same time, as we worked on it and I wrote it, Richard became thoughtful and aware of the drama, the emotional content in the scenes as well as the visuals. Tony/Norman found his arc, falling in love and losing his sanity at the same time, and terrified it was happening. To him, not Meg Tilly.

Richard and I plotted out scene by scene the changing relationship as Meg Tilly begins to care for Norman, what the actors were playing, the growing guilt, how to block them, the inserts and finally, most important of all, how to use the Hitchcock shots (think high down). Richard sketched them out, rudimentary storyboards, and I wrote them in, like the dolly into the eye staring through the hole in the wall.

In other words, Richard did *Psycho II* as if Mr. Hitchcock had done it. The only thing missing were the finished boards posted on the walls in Richard's office, and I was along for the ride. You'll see storyboards and story beats included later on in this book.

Richard Franklin: Typically, when the picture succeeded, the very same people who said it was career suicide said we couldn't have missed - that with Tony and the Bates Motel and house, it was foolproof.

I considered the endeavor precarious but was motivated by both my desire to direct in Hollywood and my sense that since they were going to make the picture anyway, it might as well be done well.

My brief was to find a writer and come up with an original story - I wasn't even allowed to read Bloch's novel, for fear I might end up on the witness stand. I interviewed about fifteen writers and was impressed by a script called *The Crystal Tower* by Tom Holland who was a client of my lawyer's. Had I seen *The Beast Within*, I might have had second thoughts, but *The Crystal Tower* was a beautiful Arthurian fantasy with great action set pieces. I reasoned that I didn't need a writer with a knowledge of thrillers, just someone with a good sense of story and the ability to write set pieces.

Tom Holland: Richard told everybody how much he loved *The Crystal Tower*. Also, the fact he actually read it, not an assistant, not a reader doing coverage, *he* read the script; do you know how unusual that is in Hollywood? For example, two days before I was to begin shooting on *Fright Night*, my first directorial effort, Guy McElaine (head of Columbia Studio at the time), called me two days before production, freaked that I had ended with Peter Vincent turning into a vampire on live TV. *Fright Night*, indeed. He insisted I change it to a happy ending. Desperate to direct my first movie, especially based on a script that I wrote and loved, I did it immediately. (Hell of a cliffhanger having that happen to Peter Vincent, wasn't it? The point is that McElaine, who had given me that proverbial "green light," had never read the script up to the point. People in Hollywood never read scripts, and only looked at the package, concept, stars, director, and budget, so knowing Richard did was a big deal to me.

About Richard's low blow about *The Beast Within*, he originally told me he considered *The Beast Within* to be a suspense piece. Maybe he just wanted to give me confidence as we bagan the project. If so, it was much needed, so thank you.

TO·LET

Chapter 5
How Could It Possibly Work?

Richard Franklin: The biggest challenge was that of targeting the audience. The picture had to work for film-buffs, for those who remembered the impact of *Psycho* and for young audiences who knew it only as television fare. What's more, every one of these groups had misconceptions, particularly about the shower scene.

Andrew London: While at USC, I happened to step in on a film class where the professor was showing the students the shower scene on a stop-and-go projector. "You see," he said, "the knife never enters the body." I pointed out that indeed it does: that you can see the tip of the knife sink into the midriff of Janet Leigh's body double a couple of inches. Hitchcock loved confounding the censors by creating his own narrative around the film and thus avoid getting censored by them. This is in line with creating the whole "No one will be seated after the film begins" ad campaign upon the release of the film.

Richard Franklin: The buffs claimed incorrectly that Hitchcock abhorred screen violence and that the scene was a model of restraint, yet older audiences remembered it as unrestrained and shockingly violent. Younger audiences on the other hand, saw the scene as fairly tame. And there was even a group of people who claimed the blood in the bath had been red (they were remembering Sam Katzman's *The Tingler*).

Andrew London: Richard is confusing Sam Katzman with that other maestro of schlock horror William Castle, who both produced and directed *The Tingler*.

Richard Franklin: In this regard, my biggest encouragement was going back to the original reviews of *Psycho* and discovering that the press universally panned the picture. The shower scene in particular, was considered "obscenely violent".

Andrew London: We would inevitably receive the same treatment from some of the critics. I remember one TV reviewer railing against the perceived violence of Vera Miles getting a knife down her throat. My fear, as I edited it, was that no one would ever buy our dummy head as anything but what it was. Tells you something about the power of suggestion!

Tom Holland: I still have the reviews. Shocking now, but they were just horrible. Uniformly so. They were with *Bonnie and Clyde*, too, so bad that Jack Warner pulled the picture. Pauline Kael gave it a rave and saved it.

Andrew London: This is a bit of an overstatement, as the film did well in the cities, but didn't get a leg up in the heartland until they tweaked the ad campaign. And Warner didn't pull it but got attacked by Beatty for his underwhelming support.

Richard Franklin: But considering the changes in the thriller genre post-Psycho, there was no way of being more violent than the form had become, so we decided not to try. We came up with a couple of shock images, but these were based on "pain" rather than gore (I would argue that a knife through the hands is much stronger than decapitation).

Tom Holland: Big yes, to the above. The two moments where we catered to the tastes of the time, the teenagers being killed, and Vera Miles being stabbed through the mouth, both in the basement. And, yes, I agree, it was a bit over the top, but those were the times of John Carpenter and Brian De Palma doing great work, even if it wasn't recognized. *The Thing* was universally panned and did little business at the time. Hard to believe now, isn't it? Hard for me, too. At the time we did *Psycho II* nobody thought that movies lasted beyond their initial release, and no matter how successful, disappeared into the yawning maw of TV only to be forgotten. This is why I am both pleasantly surprised, nee shocked, that *Psycho II* somehow began to emerge about twenty years ago as a critical success. The recent forty-year anniversary was a time for celebration of the movie as a work of art. Something that I never expected and am deeply thankful for. And the reason for this book.

Richard Franklin: Above all, however, we focused on coming up with a strong story.

When Tom was hired, I told him I already had the basis of the story. My image of Norman and "mother' on the staircase may not sound like much, but it embodied two major elements which I believe were germane to the eventual success of the picture.

The first was the idea of having Norman "come home". Bloch's sequel did not return to the motel, but it seemed to me the setting, particularly of the old dark house on the hill, was central to *Psycho*. In Freudian terms, the house represented the mother (i.e.. Norman's Superego).

Tom Holland: He's one hundred percent correct, no self-doubt here: these are leaps of genius at the moment of creation, and they were Richard's. They were also visually right, and Richard was nothing if not visual. Take a look at *Road Games* to see.

Richard Franklin: *Psycho* had been set mostly in the Motel (Norman's Id), but the house interested me more. The famous still of Norman, with the house looming over him in silhouette, had become the quintessential *Psycho* image, even though it was a publicity shot and did not appear in the original. We would end *Psycho II* with a variation of this image.

Andrew London: It was this image that we used in our holiday card to cast and crew that would become our indelible poster image. The studio presented us with three rather lackluster poster images, all with a rather awkwardly worded tagline. I said we had a perfectly useful image from our holiday card, which was the final shot of the film, and stated what would become our tagline: "It's 22 years later, and Norman Bates is coming home."

Tom Holland: The image above is the basis for everything that followed, Richard and Andrew saw it. There was no motel nor, more importantly, a *Psycho* house before us on the lot, not since the original, and that had been dismantled years previous and reused on the lot so many times it was no longer recognizable.

Richard Franklin: The second decision was that of bringing "mother" back (not an easy task when one considered she died ten years prior to the original). But this challenge was the basis of most of the plot twists in *Psycho II* and allowed us to make the picture more than just a sequel.

I had admired Nicholas Meyer's treatment of Sherlock Holmes' childhood in *The Seven Percent Solution,* and it occurred to me that if we changed the back story of the original and introduced the possibility that Mrs Bates might not have been Norman's real mother, we could bring her back from the dead as it were. This would allow us to change the original without actually touching it.

Tom Holland: I can't remember who thought of what, but we agreed on 22 years later, the use of the *Psycho* house and the motel. What Richard was doing was what directors do, thinking of how to put the film in visual terms. I was worrying about continuity and what was going on inside the characters, what was driving them to what turns out to be a tragedy.

But we somehow got to the opening scene, Vera Miles going off in court as Norman is released from the mental institution, and what that portends, and his coming back to THE HOUSE after 22 years. Norman holding on to his sanity, which is under constant and ascending assault, is me. But I arranged them to echo the moments both of us, Richard and I, loved as we watched Hitchcock's oeuvre, in today's terms, the kills.

I remember the "real" Mom being my idea, so I could justify the madness that was happening, but it was more important to trace Norman's mental and spiritual decay. Tony read it and loved it

Richard Franklin: We worked at Tom's house in Benedict Canyon, plotting the picture by pinning index cards to a notice board in his living room, while I paced up and down explaining the rules of Hitchcockian suspense. I hoped to get under the guard of our would-be detractors reasoning it would be better to have too much plot than not enough. I figured that if we made it hard for our would-be critics, they would have to keep up with a complex plot before they could pooh-pooh the picture.

Tom Holland: I also had learned enough about Hollywood by that time, multiple writers, multiple drafts, and endless credit arbitrations, so I wrote both *The Beast Within* and *Psycho II* as thrillers, with driving plot lines. If it worked, and I'd like to think both scripts did, it made it harder for the studio to rewrite me without throwing the entire script out. In other words, when the story is highly plotted, the guy who is rewriting you is pretty much limited to dialogue and supposedly character, but it's hard to change enough of the story to get co-screenplay credit. Hollywood is killer, isn't it?

Richard Franklin: So each time Tom and I agreed on a basic plot point, I would say, "Well the normal scene to follow would be such and such, so how can we do the opposite?"

Tom Holland: I remember writing into visuals, shots already selected by Richard and me trying to put the shots to work in a coherent manner. To that end, Richard and I watched EVERY ONE OF Mr. Hitchcock's films, me studying how he built the suspense, Richard looking at the individual shots in a sequence that quite often ended with a shocking reveal.

Richard Franklin: Secrecy was vital. Cast and crew were asked to treat the story as "top secret," and for fun, I did as we had done on *Patrick* and withheld the ending of the script. On *Patrick*, we hadn't known what the ending would be, but this time we closed the set to shoot the scene and even had preview screenings which ended with a title card saying that our ending would not be revealed till the release of the picture.

Andrew London: I don't recall this at all. Perhaps there was a screening, with the last shot being the silhouette of a woman climbing the stairs to the house?

Tom Holland: Not that I remember.

Richard Franklin: In this way, I reasoned nobody would tell a story without the "punch-line".

Tom Holland: Richard told me Mr. Hitchcock had done the same thing with *Psycho I*. Whew, I can't believe I have to put a number on the original *Psycho* now.

Richard Franklin: Tom and I were trying to work out how to bring Norman's mother back when I realized that the woman in the periwinkle blue dress with white hair in a bun, was a stylistic conceit on Hitchcock's part. If she looked like that at the time of her death ten years earlier, she had to be Norman's grandmother.

Tom came up with the Mrs Spool idea, about which I was ecstatic. Not only did it allow the sort of twist to the original I was after, but it gave a new explanation to Norman's psychosis. Making Mrs Bates the "wicked stepmother" from a Grimm fairytale mitigated Norman's matricide and partially explained it. The idea of murder with a blunt instrument and no cuts (of either kind) was mine -the antithesis of the shower murder. Tom supplied the coal shovel.

Andrew London: Of course, there were cuts. Nobody was going to hit our actress over the head, even with a rubber shovel, in one take, and expect her to react realistically to getting, literally, "clobbered". There are three shots and two edits: Norman just hits Mrs. Spool, and we cut on the impact and sound effect to our dummy getting hit and starting to collapse, then back to our actress falling to the ground in a high angle. There's also the suggestion, at least in the edit, that Norman has poisoned her with the tea as well, allowing for the shock and surprise of the shovel over the head.

Tom Holland: I was on the set, watching Richard set up the final scene with Mrs. Spool. I had written it with Norman poisoning her, but it was weak. The ending, not the tea. It didn't finish with a "bang," as they say, and we needed a murder weapon that would do that and might just possibly be in the kitchen, you know, sitting inside the door to the backyard. That's right, the shovel.

Doesn't every kitchen have one?

Actors Anthony Perkins and Robert Loggia (partially blocked) with Richard Franklin at Mother's opened graveside

Chapter 6
Replicating The Past

Richard Franklin: I deliberately avoided running *Psycho* because I wanted to sequelize the movie in my mind; the one that had scared the dickens out of me as a twelve-year-old, rather than the classic it had become. In any case, I had seen *Psycho* so many times (at least fifty) I could run it in my head whenever I wanted. So instead, I ran some of the expressionist works that had influenced the young Hitchcock. We looked at Murnau's *The Last Laugh, Nosferatu,* and *Sunrise.* Also, Pabst's *Joyless Street* and *Secrets of the Soul.*

Tom Holland: And more, we ran EVERY Hitchcock film from the silents through Family Plot, looking at every suspense sequence and its climax. That as well as the German expressionists who had influenced Hitchcock himself. We broke out camera moves, like at the orchestra in Young and Innocent, where Mr. Hitchcock dollies in on the twitching eye. That became the push in on Tony in the opening shot as Vera Miles goes off on him in the courtroom.

Richard Franklin: I screened *Psycho* only once for my key people (although there was a print and several videotapes available to them at all times). It was instead Stanley Cortez's astonishing imagery for Charles Laughton's *Night of the Hunter* which I told Dean Cundey had the look I was after. In fact, *Night of the Hunter* directly influenced the murder in the fruit cellar and the pull back out of Mary's bedroom at the end of the second act.

Tom Holland: That's a vignette, the central image surrounded by black, and I thought Richard had pulled it from the silent films we had screened. I must look at *Night of the Hunter* again. Stanley Cortez, who shot it, was considered the master of B&W.

Guy Green, Academy Award-winning DP on David Lean's *Great Expectation*, wasn't bad either. I was the juvenile in *Walk in the Spring Rain* that he directed. What an experience. Starred Anthony Quinn and Ingrid Bergman. I got to kiss her, and Tony got jealous. Bruce Lee was the stunt coordinator. The movie wasn't a hit but was a high point in my life as an actor.

Now why would I be talking about another movie when I'm writing about *Psycho II*? Because my mother in *Walk in the Spring Rain* was played by the very talented Virginia Gregg, who also provided the voice of Mother in the original *Psycho, Psycho II,* and *Psycho III*. She was a huge voiceover radio artist. Mr. Hitchcock must have agreed because he cast her (voice) in the original *Psycho,* and then in *Walk in the Spring Rain,* she ends up playing my on-screen mother.

When I discovered the tie-in, it spun me about. Coincidence, fate, ten degrees of separation, I don't know, but it made me feel like I was tied to *Psycho* in ways I had never understood.

Richard Franklin: Unlike *Patrick* it was never my intention to imitate Hitchcock's style, but rather to do variations on a theme. I was greatly encouraged when I realized the extent to which Hitchcock himself had been influenced by Murnau: not only does *Sunrise* begin with the same transition from artwork to reality that Hitchcock used in *North by Northwest,* but the murder scene is underscored with Gounod's *Funeral March of a Marionette* (Hitchcock's theme from the television show). I began to feel as if I was working in a tradition rather than plundering the tomb of an idol. I was also encouraged by fellow Australian Percy Grainger's variations on *Porgy and Bess.*

Much thought was given to the question of whether to shoot in color. Hitchcock claimed the only reason he shot the original in B&W, was to tone down the blood in the shower (And seeing Gus van Sant's remake, he was right), yet *Psycho* had become a classic of B&W cinematography. Universal did not want a B&W picture and was not interested in my idea of shooting on color negative, making the theatrical prints in B&W then releasing it on television in color. What finally made me decide color was right for the picture was the number of buffs who came to see me, insisting we should shoot in B&W, but asking if I had found the color tests Hitchcock was supposed to have shot for the shower scene (such tests never existed).

Tom Holland: If you want to be a director, think visually, often to the point of obsession; knowing how to tell a story or work with actors doesn't hurt either.

Richard Franklin: I had always believed that the same stylization is possible in color as in B&W. However, to get a B&W look in color, cameramen usually go for muted tones, soft lighting, fog, and diffusion. To me, this is the antithesis of B&W, which is high in contrast. Indeed, the early Technicolor three-strip process actually used B&W stock. I showed Dean my favorite example of three-strip Technicolor, the *Limehouse Blues* number from *Ziegfeld Follies* (actually shot on the B&W sets for *Dorian Gray*), and told him this was the way I wanted the color of *Psycho II* to look.

Tom Holland: This was one of the great things about working with Richard. I got to see lots of old movies, many of them silent, in the screening rooms at Universal. You must remember that this was just as VHS and Beta were fighting it out, and cable was just being strung. It was hard to impossible to watch old movies. There was NO WAY of seeing them for the public, and at the time, that was me.

Now you can't NOT see content.

Richard Franklin: Our next problem was that of duplicating the sets. Incredibly, neither Paramount nor Universal had blueprints, so my Art Director, John Corso, had to freeze a videotape of the movie and literally count the number of steps up to the house. In this regard, Hitchcock's guided tour trailer for *Psycho* was more helpful than the movie itself. There was also a published picture book of *Psycho* which was a great help.

Tom Holland: I met with Henry Bumstead, Academy Award-winning production designer, and went with him to the department where all the blueprints were kept on the Universal lot. There we found the designs for the house. Which was NOT standing at the time, at least in no recognizable way, the motel decades gone. Can you imagine the Universal lot before the *Psycho* house and City Walk? I can. I saw it. The hills at the back of the lot were bare in 1982, although they had started to put in an outdoor amphitheater.

Richard Franklin: We imagined Universal's prop store would be full of memorabilia, but most of the pieces had been sold or stolen. Our set dresser Jennifer Polito did an incredible detective job, locating almost every key piece needed.

No color production stills exist from *Psycho* and Hilton could not remember the colors of the sets. I had to go on instinct, reasoning that the entrance hall of the Bates house would resemble the McKittrick Hotel in *Vertigo* and that green would be prevalent in the mother's room. Apparently, we got it right, because early in the shoot Joe Hurley, the Art Director of the original, visited the set and described the experience as one of deja-vu.

Tom Holland: It was to me, too, and by that time, I was submerged in *Psycho* minutiae, but seeing the house go up with the stairs and the motel was amazing. It was everything Richard had talked about while I wrote the script. I could see what he was seeing.

In or about that time the Art Dept. did a beautiful scale model of the *Psycho* house. I could see the angles and the framing Richard had been talking about for weeks. I was learning how to storyboard because I wanted to see the shots as I wrote. Look at the dissolves, the cuts between scenes, the vignetting, the crane shots in and around the house. That was all thought of before Richard started to shoot.

The house was the stage for *Psycho II*, but Tony Perkins was its beating heart, and Meg Tilly gave us somebody to worry about without feeling guilty. Same with Norman, but here there's a bit of guilt. After all, you're worried about a serial murderer who is slowly losing his sanity. The viewer is falling inside Norman's head and feeling sorry for him because, you know from *Psycho I* he was traumatized by his mother, but you don't know how. Hopefully, *Psycho II* answered some of those questions.

FAIRVALE IV BANK & TRUST
ANTIQUES
ANTIQUES
Halloween
RICHARD FRANKLIN

Chapter 7
The Team

Richard Franklin: I was keen to use as many people who had been involved in the original picture as possible. Clearly Janet Leigh was out of the question, though many people have asked why I didn't find a part for Martin Balsam (who also died in the original).

I approached Simon Oakland to reprise his role as the psychologist, but the poor man was obviously very ill and died soon afterward. John McIntyre would have been our sheriff, but the Universal casting department screwed up, and he took another part (I did, however, use him in *Cloak & Dagger*, also written by Tom Holland).

Tom Holland: *Cloak & Dagger* was an experience, too.

Richard Franklin: Vera Miles initially refused us, but Hilton persuaded her to read the script, and after doing so, she drove down from Big Bear to meet me. Such was her fervor about the insanity plea that I used Vera's own words in the courtroom scene.

Tom Holland: I gave Vera something to play in the script, the vengeance-driven sister, and she proceeded to make it come alive. Her Hitchcock and Ford stories were incredible. She was to play the lead in Vertigo but was pregnant and lost the part to Kim Novak. She was also a total pro, even if she was still upset about that.

There was a sense of family to the set because Hilton Green had made sure to bring back as many people who worked with Mr. Hitchcock (nobody called him Hitch to his face) as possible. The script supervisor, dresser, Edith Head was next door on the lot. What I'd written was coming alive, and being shot *just* as I wrote it. (Hint, work closely with the director) I couldn't believe any of it, especially after my first experience on *The Beast Within* where I was banned from seeing the dailies. Richard even cast me as one of the Deputies and I got my best friend since high school, Chris Hendrie, cast as the other deputy. The experience was a dream come true for both of us and I can't think of a bad moment.

Well, a few, but I'm not going to talk about them.

Richard Franklin: Behind the scenes too, I was keen to use people who had a connection with Hitchcock. Hitchcock's chauffeur Tony and various others who were still working on the Universal lot were employed, and our wardrobe mistress was the daughter of *Psycho*'s script supervisor.

Peggy Robertson, Hitchcock's personal assistant for many years, came in, and I was very keen to employ her, but I surmise there was a rivalry between Hilton and her, and it didn't happen. She did, however tell me Hitchcock's idea of a dolly into a peephole hidden in a flower petal on a wall of floral wallpaper, and I resolved to incorporate this shot in our obligatory shower scene.

For the part of Mary, Jamie Lee Curtis was an obvious choice, but I talked with her, and we agreed it was too obvious. In any case, she wanted to go in other career directions, and her presence would have tipped our hand plot-wise. I met with Kathleen Turner and Carrie Fisher, both of whom were interested. Kathleen would have been too strong for Norman and Carrie convinced me we needed an unknown.

Tom Holland: I went through several of these meetings with Richard. They were all strong actresses, but it really went on who could play the girl that he, Norman, would take into the house (yes, that house), that he would feel safe with. Meg Tilly had that naturalness and innocence, and you would not have thought she could be part of Lila Crane's attempt to drive Norman mad again. But then she was Meg's mother. Mothers are a big part of the problem in the *Psycho* legacy, aren't they?

Richard Franklin: As unknown or lesser actresses went, an extremely attractive actress named Faye Grant would probably have been Hitchcock's choice, but (like Kathleen) we could not have believed she would be taken in by Norman. Lisa Eilbacher came back three times and even read with Tony. But finally, I decided to be courageous and go with relatively unknown Meg Tilly.

A former dancer, who had injured her back and decided to take up acting instead, Meg had a fey innocence which I felt suggested the female equivalent of the young Norman. At the time, she had been in only two pictures, Disney's *Tex* and a cheapie called *One Dark Night*, yet her older sister Jennifer (who would become the better-known of the two) was still unheard of. I consider my casting of her something of a coup since it preceded *The Big Chill* and her Academy nomination in *Agnes of God*.

Anthony Perkins (Norman Bates)

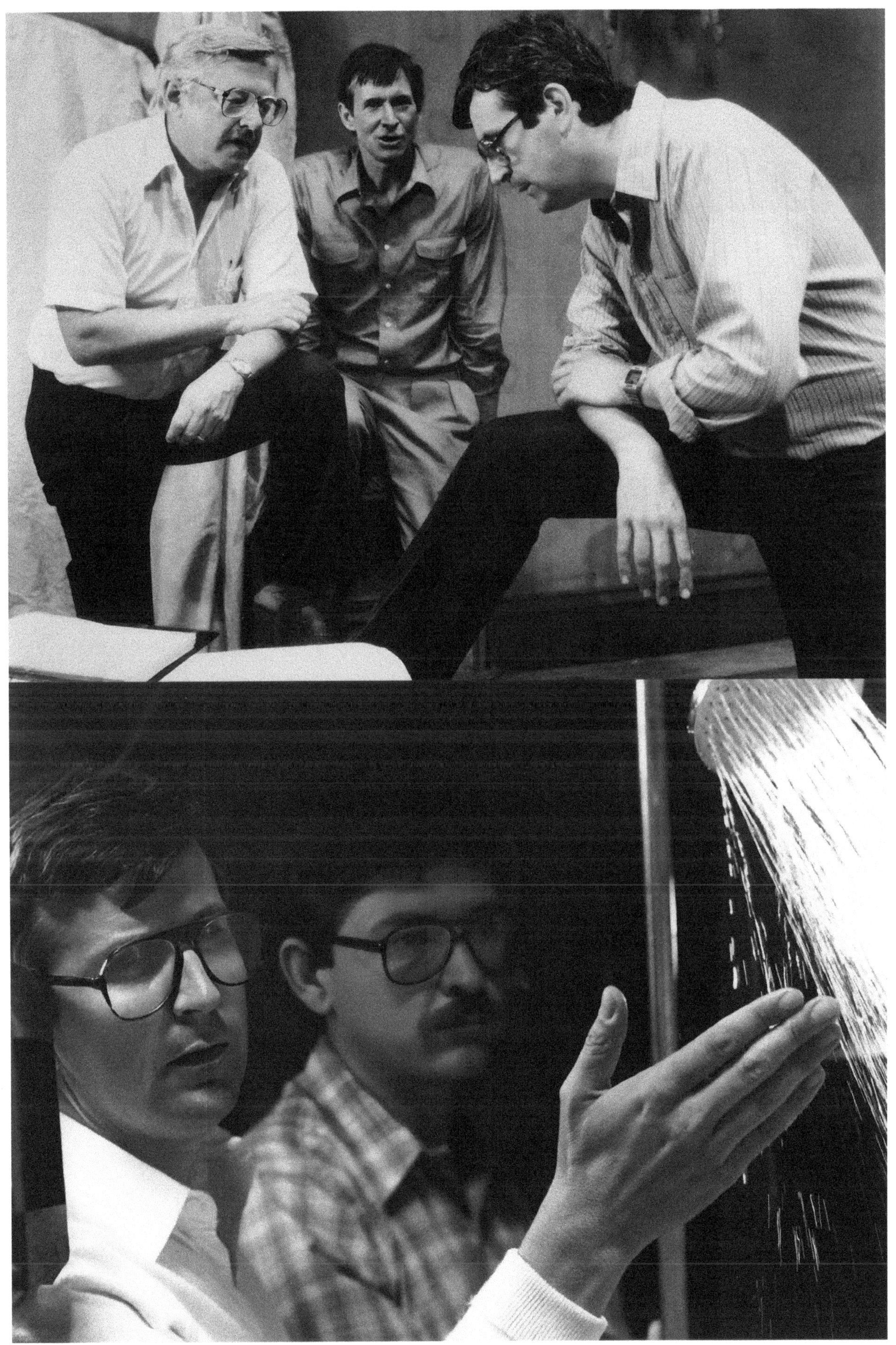

TOP: *Producer Hilton Green with Perkins and Franklin *
BOTTOM: *Franklin and 1st AD Don Zepfel preparing for the shower scene*

Robert Loggia (Dr. Bill Raymond)

Dennis Franz (Warren Toomey)

TOP: Meg Tilly (Mary Loomis) with Perkins
BOTTOM: Holland and Chris Hendrie (Deputy Pool)

Chapter 8
Shooting Memories

Richard Franklin: I don't believe I had even seen the giant Chapman Titan crane before my first day on *Psycho II*, however for the first shot I climbed aboard to film Tony and Bob Loggia walking up the hill to the house. Later in the shoot, I wanted to crane from the oval window at the top of the house to the basement and was shocked when I arrived to find the camera department rehearsing with a Louma crane mounted on top of a Titan crane.

Orson Welles described Hollywood as the best model train a kid ever got to play with. Certainly, he had fun with a Chapman crane.

Another challenge was the schedule of 30 days. The original had been shot in 32, of which five or six were spent in the shower, so I couldn't complain. However, having spent close to 60 days on *Roadgames*, I wasn't quite sure how I'd accomplish the task. I met with Don Siegel, who apart from being Clint Eastwood's directing tutor, had several early credits shot at a blistering pace (*Invasion of the Body Snatchers* was shot in 14 days).

Andrew London: Actually it was 23 days.

Richard Franklin: He told me the key to shooting fast, was to start fast and not to give the camera department the luxury of multiple takes. I took his advice and the minute a shot was acceptable from a performance point of view, I moved on without so much as asking the operator whether he'd got it on film. Near the end of shooting, he thanked me for the boost in self-confidence he felt this approach had given him.

Or perhaps someone was watching over us..... Later, when we assembled the cast and crew on the staircase for the customary unit photograph, I included a small cardboard Hitchcock silhouette (which was used to cast a shadow for his appearance early in the picture).

Tom Holland: You saw it in a wide shot of the room where, before the lights are turned on, you can see the unforgettable Hitchcock silhouette on the armoire in the right of frame.

I like to think the overwhelming respect Richard and I showed to Mr. Hitchcock and the original *Psycho* disarmed the critics a bit. Everything I used to build the script was based on facts given in the original. I was trying to root *Psycho II* to the first *Psycho*, because it worked dramatically, and I thought it might be some protection from the negative critical reception we were expecting.

Richard Franklin: Tony Perkins was extremely obliging and easy to direct - which was generous considering his desire to direct himself. An intellectual and stickler for precise language, I often had to resort to a thesaurus to give him exactly the right shading for an emotion. But he was always eager to please and cheerful. When we were shooting one of my customary high-angle shots of a scene with Bob Loggia, Tony asked me if I realized I was shooting a scene between "two men with boot polish on their heads".

Tom Holland: I was an actor in a bygone age, working under the AKA of Tom Fielding, since Tom Holland was then in use in SAG at the time (and still is).

It was a movie with Ingrid Bergman and Anthony Quinn who told me he was putting color on his bald spot and someday I'd do it, too. Gave me the formula George Raft had given him. It was turpentine mixed with shoe polish, but I can't remember the proportions. LOL Too bad, I could use it now.

Richard Franklin: Vera too, was a real pro. As an actress, she literally knocked my socks off, particularly in the bar scene with Meg. Having alternated between both of my favorite directors, she had many stories about the practical jokes played by Hitchcock and John Ford.

When we did the shot of her entering the cellar to the house, I told her she would have to climb into the tiny space under the sloping doors and crouch till I called cut. But once she was inside, I called "Lunch!" On another occasion, she had to scuttle about on her back crab fashion, for take after take on a cement floor with an enormous knife sticking out of her mouth. After many jokes at her expense, she finally broke up and in spite of the mouthful, managed to blurt out "Damn you Hitch!"

Tom Holland: I wonder what Vera Miles really thought. We went gory in a few spots, here and the kids in the wood bin. It was the times, and we didn't want to be too tame. Robert Bloch criticized me for gratuitous violence at a symposium we did at the WGA after the movie opened.

He was right, but as I said they were the times, and there was pressure to make it visceral.

However, the scene that really knocked the audience out of their chairs was the end; Norman killing Mrs. Spool with the shovel was a real shocker.

Richard Franklin: In spite of her talent, Meg had no confidence in her abilities at all. Vera railed at her for being so inwardly focused in their scenes together and Tony became so exasperated he went to the Universal hierarchy and asked for her to be recast. Incredibly, Meg had never seen *Psycho* and would ask questions like "How come Tony is always being treated like the star of this movie?"

Tom Holland: I can't believe she'd never seen the original Psycho. But then she is an actress.

Per above, I watched Meg and Vera Miles shoot the scene in the bar in the back lot small town, where their plot is revealed, and Meg's hesitation to follow through. Vera drove the scene, but it was the intensity of back and forth in the moment that Vera and Tony were talking about. They wanted an actor that gave them more to play off of, to react to.

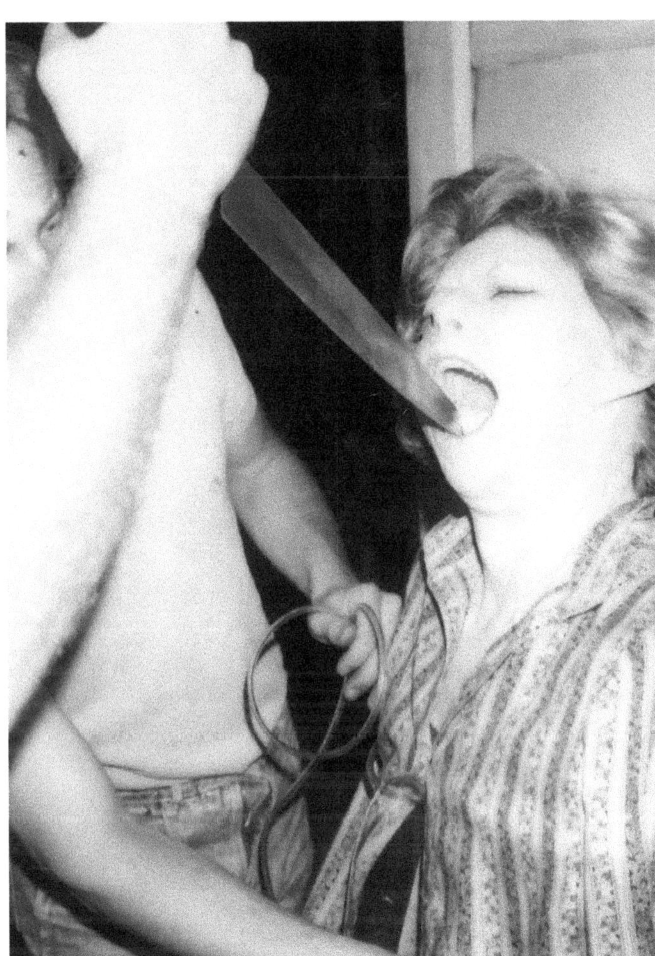

Richard Franklin: Apart from this, the shoot was completed on schedule, the wrap party being held on Hitchcock's birthday. So happy was everybody, that the crew actually presented plaques to the producers and myself - in my experience, this is without precedent.

Tom Holland: I'd forgotten about the plaques. Richard did a brilliant job, and as he said Hilton Green totally protected him. But Hilton also understood what he was doing. He had been Hitch's First AD for 25 years. Richard designed the sets for the shots. I worked it out with him, he drew it out or showed me a Hitchcock film with the camera move he was looking for and how to adjust for the drama I was writing. Richard was riffing off the Master by using his sets that made all those overheads seem so right.

The script just got tighter and tighter in terms of the emotional moments and the rising suspense cues, especially the latter. It matched the rising pressure on Norman as he became increasingly desperate – and unhinged.

Perkins with wife Berry Berenson

Chapter 9
...And That's a Wrap

Richard Franklin: Immediately after shooting, I took a couple of weeks off and went to Australia, where the family had gone during the shoot. Although I like to leave the editor alone to do his first cut unsupervised, I was eager to have Andrew London's reaction as soon as he had it put together. He commented that the picture struck him as a critical "thesis" on *Psycho* (which is probably the way I now view it).

Tom Holland: Andrew, what did you mean by "critical thesis."

Andrew London: I don't recall using the term at all. But perhaps a story from the editing room would answer that. Richard was then in Australia, leaving me completely alone and, with the time difference and the difficulty of international phone connections, I didn't have the ability to call him up with a question in the moment. So, I was editing the sequence where Norman enters Mother's room to find it dressed and set as if she had just been there, but in reality our unknown tormenter had set it up in this fashion. The material shot for this scene appeared to me to be a series of random shots of Norman touching objects, moving about the room and opening the wardrobe, and I could not make sense of how it was meant to go together. But, I figured the answer might lay somewhere within the body of the original *Psycho*. As I had a print of the film in the editing room, I rolled down through each reel until I hit paydirt: Richard had replicated shot-for-shot a similar sequence in the original film, so I had my model. I measured each shot, analyzing the cutting points and shot lengths, and proceeded to assemble the cut. With only a slight difference in one shot that had a minor camera move that did not appear in the original, the sequence in *Psycho II* is an exact replica.

Richard Franklin: We screened the picture first for Verna Fields (the editor of *Jaws* whom Universal had promoted to Vice President).

Andrew London: We told Verna we would screen it for her, and her alone, at the wrap party (which we held on the *Psycho II* set). Her reaction was one of complete girlish delight. She remained a steadfast booster for the film, even sending us notes from her hospital room, where she kept a video player to view the changes. I remain forever grateful to Verna as, when I knew the studio was trying to get Richard to hire one of its veteran editors for the film, I requested a meeting with her in her office at Universal. At the time, I was supervising the sound mix on Wim Wenders' *Hammett* and was allowed to leave to make my appointment. At the end of our meeting, she told me: "Well, I think the director should get the editor of his choice, and, besides, sound editors make the best editors!" (She was once a sound editor herself with such credits as *El Cid* and *A Face in The Rain*.)

Richard Franklin: She said it was the most polished rough cut she'd ever seen and offered to persuade the studio to spend more on getting the composer of my choice Jerry Goldsmith. Regrettably, Verna was dying of cancer, and viewing *Psycho II* was the last thing she did before going to the hospital. Andrew and I sent her a card with a frame of Vera with the knife through her head, and believing Verna had only a back condition, our caption read "Things could be worse"

Andrew London: Actually, it was: "Cheer up. Things could be worse!".

Richard Franklin: We never heard Verna's response since she never came out of the hospital.

Andrew London: On the contrary, when we eventually heard what she was in the hospital for, we expressed our dismay to Verna's assistant at what we wrote, possibly upsetting her. She said: "Not at all. She had a good laugh."

We screened my cut to the then-head of Universal, Ned Tanen, who tried to remain nonchalant and detached, but literally fell out of his chair near the end of the screening.

Tom Holland: Bet it was the shovel scene; knocked everybody out of their chair, including Mrs. Loomis.

Richard Franklin: From this point on, the "buzz" at the studio began to build, and when lunchtime screenings were arranged for Universal employees, people flocked to see it.

Tom Holland: This is every writer/director/editor/creative person's, dream. You can't believe they love it (me, my work, Sally Field, move over). It's a rush of exhilaration, a high unlike any other, with all kinds of great (and terrible) things happening. What's amazing is this was spontaneous within the studio, word of mouth being the final driver of movie success. Novels, too, so much art is finally sold by people enjoying it and telling others. Marketing just gets the word of mouth going in the first place– or kills it.

Richard Franklin: Hilton brought "Father Tom", the priest who had given Hitchcock the last rights, to the cast and crew screening, and he announced it was "better than the original". I suggested this was "sacrilege," and he said "Nonsense, I'll summon Hitch up - I'm sure he'll agree."

As in Australia, my first experience with the marketing people was a nightmare. The head of the department claimed they'd done market research which indicated "92% of the core audience don't know the original picture". I asked to see the research and he called in a secretary who corrected him: the awareness of *Psycho* was higher than *Star Wars*. One can only wonder where he got the spurious statistic and how the picture would have been sold had I not challenged it.

One executive presented an idea for a trailer with great gusto. He said he had "a vision" - "of rain on a windscreen and the SWISH SWISH of wipers revealing the Motel sign". I pointed out he had re-invented a scene from the original picture.

These people went on to spend over $12m launching a picture which cost less than $4m to produce. $100,000 alone was spent getting a dozen artists to come up with one-sheet concepts which were all thrown out - not surprising when the publicity department, in their wisdom, would not allow them to see the film.

The ad that was finally used was the last frame of the picture, part painted by Albert Whitlock and used by our office as a Christmas card during post-production.

Tom Holland: Albert Whitlock was a genius. Last of the great painters. But the opening shot in *Fright Night* by Richard Edlund wasn't bad. Nor was the artistry of John DeCuir, a brilliant production designer. And I thought the budget was just a little under 5 million.

Richard Franklin: The "22 years later" copy line was mine, slipped anonymously into an IN basket in the publicity department.

Andrew London: As stated earlier, I suggested the line when they showed their poster tests to us. So, I don't know where he came up with this anonymous submission idea.

Tom Holland: LOL Everybody wants to take credit. Especially directors if it's a success. And everybody flees failure, ergo the expression that it is an orphan. I've experienced both (never solely my fault, of course) and so did Richard. The trick is bouncing back, which of course becomes more difficult with the passage of time, not just because one outgrows the core movie-going audience which at the time was from adolescence to late twenties. In other words, you're losing touch with your core audience with every passing year, but also just the sheer physical demands of actually getting through a schedule that can run from 22 days to a year and a half, longer now with post-CGI. If you work in a genre like horror you're bound to be shooting a lot of nights which when I started out was doing a turnaround from day to night at least once a week. That meant that every week ended at dawn on Saturday and then you had to be up at dawn on Monday to begin day shooting again. Depending on the split between day and night you could be doing turnarounds twice a week or more.

Killer.

Chapter 10
The Preview

Richard Franklin: As the June opening approached, I flew with the family to Delaware where our in-laws were staying on a university exchange program. Leaving Rebecca with them, we took Davey and Den's mother by train for their first trip to NYC. Universal supplied an opulent suite at The Sherry Netherland and numerous house seats to Broadway shows between interviews etc..

Tom Holland: Same thing happened to me with the opening of *Fright Night*. Ah, the good old days. Also happened with *Cloak & Dagger*, the next film that Richard and I did, which was produced by Allan Carr. He also produced *La Cage aux* Folles on Broadway. Needless to say, when I went to N.Y.C. I was comped to that play and several others. Great times.

Below Richard talks about Andrew Sarris. He loved truly great film critics, Robin Wood, and many others. It was also the time of Pauline Kael. A big chunk of Richard was an academic. In fact, he spent his last years teaching film students in Australia. He was a great teacher. (Look at me; big smile) But what always comes through is his love of film.

Richard Franklin: On the evening of the NY press preview, I met Andrew Sarris for drinks. His book *The American Cinema* had been a favorite of mine for some years, and I believed his reviews for *The Village Voice* to be extremely influential (the newspaper having little readership outside NYC is an obvious one for other critics to steal from.) We talked in a bar a short distance from the theatre until about fifteen minutes prior to the screening, and the lobbying paid off with an excellent review. But as we left the bar, we were greeted with a sight indelibly etched on my mind.

Tom Holland: This is amazing. Can you imagine what Richard was feeling? The previews had been enough for me. Seattle, Century City, wherever: the results were uniformly excellent. You could hear it in the audience reacting in all the right places, especially the shovel killing Mrs. Spool at the end. Dead silence, followed by a hubbub as the audience recovered. And it was a spur-of-the-moment grab as Richard, and I realized that poisoning her wasn't enough.

For the first few days after the opening, I checked the lines in Westwood which were always long, but by that time I had turned to other projects. I was the writer. The director always gets the glamour. Fine with me, but the director also takes the abuse and must get through the struggle of getting his vision on film which was a battle more often than not. I was blessed that my first directorial effort, Fright Night, was also a dream. I thank Jerry Baerwitz, who was the line producer and supported me and made all the difference. The truth is, most producers work for the studio because their eye is always on the next deal, the next movie, and not the one they are currently making.

The point is that directing is a very different process than being the writer and I wasn't as emotionally involved because I didn't understand what writing a big successful movie in Hollywood meant. *Psycho II* was about to change our lives, Richard's, and mine.

Richard Franklin: We stepped out onto Broadway a couple of blocks north of Times Square to find it literally filled with people all the way to the theatre. Traffic was stopped on the "Great White Way" as police tried to hold onlookers back so that Tony and others (my wife included) could reach the theatre by limo.

From this moment, my memories are somewhat hazy… It must have taken me close to half an hour to elbow my way to the plate glass doors of the theatre and persuade a dubious usherette to admit me. I have a sense of the time only because I left the bar fifteen minutes before showtime and by the time I found Denise in the back row of the theatre, Norman was already arguing with Toomey (about fifteen minutes into the movie). The next two or three days are similarly hazy.

After the screening, we went to Studio 54 where they decorated the discotheque for "Norman Bates Night". We were to have the place for an hour before they opened the doors to the public. One entered through a sort of "haunted house" corridor with doors opening into shower stalls complete with water and naked girls playing corpses. I honestly don't remember whether all this was in good or bad taste, since Hilton and myself had been taken to a back door and had great difficulty trying to persuade a particularly surly bouncer to let us in. My only other recollections of that night are cutting a cake in the shape of the *Psycho* house, meeting Patricia Hitchcock, who thanked me for being reverential to her father's memory and being introduced by Tony to Andy Warhol, whom I couldn't hear. Then Den and I forsook the bright lights and loud music for dinner at "21" with Bernie and the investors.

The following day I remember a sense of invulnerability as I walked along Fifth Avenue - of literally "floating" a foot above the pavement. That night, I stood in the rain and watched the crowds stretching around the block and joined the queue to attend a midnight screening with an almost entirely black audience who seemed to get every subtlety in the piece.

A few days later, we took the family to Washington, before returning to Hollywood and as I sat on the lawn, I felt this great land had taken me to its bosom.

Tom Holland: So much of this is the same as the *Fright Night*'s NYC debut and I was in a very similar fog. What can I say? Success is never what we think it will be. At least it wasn't for me. It changed so much externally, but I was still the same person with the same insecurities and self-doubt and anxiety. However, it does make it easier to afford psychological therapy, even if it didn't help me much.

Chapter 11
The Legacy

Richard Franklin: *Psycho II* grossed $8.3 million on its opening weekend.

Andrew London: No. 2 behind *Return of the Jedi*, and $13.5m in the first week. It would go on to become Universal's most profitable picture for the year, with international rentals in excess of $40m (more than the first *Psycho*).

Richard Franklin: I am often asked if I ever sensed Hitchcock's presence on the set and while I am not big on the occult, I recall the scene where Tony climbs the interior stairs for the first time. To this day the unreality of directing Tony Perkins on those sets has not entirely penetrated, but as Tony came up the stairs towards me for the first time, I had a sense of something otherworldly. Perhaps it was just a sense of deja-vu, Tony Perkins and the Psycho house being as quintessentially Hollywood as Bogart on the set of Rick's. Or perhaps someone was watching over us.

Tom Holland: Beautifully written, and I never lost my awe either walking the *Psycho* set. But when you are in production, when you are shooting, you don't have time to second-guess yourself. You do that when you're writing. LOL However, of all the movies I have written, I've never had a movie that came alive from the page to the screen quite the way *Psycho II* did. It not only echoed the first one, but it went deeper into character. The film was faithful to *Psycho* and the *Psycho II* script I had written, and I'm forever thankful.

Richard Franklin: I am sometimes disappointed that the experience of "floating down Fifth Avenue" has not come again (though, of course, I am grateful to have had it once.) And that the two further sequels (one directed by Tony) rendered the unassailable task I had undertaken merely one of a "string of sausages". But for me, the major achievement with *Psycho II* comes every time I hear someone refer to Hitchcock's classic not by its proper name but as *Psycho ONE*.

Tom Holland: Bravo to everyone involved in the making of *Psycho II*, thank you, and I wish Richard was here to share this. And thank you, Andrew London, for your telling contributions.

Now for a summing up, obviously impossible since I am still working and have no idea how this all ends. I know, death which must visit us all, is getting closer to knocking on my door (hey, what did you expect? I write tales of horror and fear and death is probably the only true companion I can count on).

But how did *Psycho II* change my life? A short story. Richard, I, and the execs from Universal were at a screening in Century City in L.A... It was a huge success with the audience. The preview cards were great and Bob Rehme, head of the studio, turned to me and asked "So what's the movie you are going to direct?

I didn't have any answer. After trying since the early nineteen seventies to get into the business, to get work as a writer, to get a movie made, and then when *The Beast Within* sank without a trace, to get a successful movie made that would get the notice of Hollywood. Then the job I had taken out of financial desperation, the movie that everybody told me was the kiss of death, *Psycho II*, looked to be a huge success. Amazing, stunning, and totally unexpected by me. You'd think I could have had a great feeling of satisfaction and be looking forward to a flood of offers, but no, that wasn't it at all.

Instead, my anxiety, low key till then, after all, what did I have to lose, exploded. Oh, no, I had to do it again and again and again. Somebody, quick, shoot me. I had seen enough during production, pre, and post, to know the pressure on the director was huge, and worse with every dollar and day you went over budget (and you were always under budgeted, and the schedule was never long enough). Richard had protected me from that because he had become as committed to the script as I was.

Also, I had strong scripts like *Border Crossing* and *The Crystal Tower* waiting in the wings. But something I could confidently direct, sure of success, in a business where there was never certainty? After all, not only does the script have to be excellent, but the casting has to be spot on, and everybody from crew to actors has to pull in the same direction. That's impossible to guarantee. All you can do is work as hard as possible and pray. Pray for what? A lot of luck because you're going to need as much as you can get.

Writing is a solitary profession. The only one you can depend on is yourself and I for one am hardly ever satisfied with my scripts or novels, short stories, or novellas, not to mention the movies and TV shows I have directed. My worst most destructive critic is myself.

So, no, Mr. Rehme, I didn't have that script and in reaction to Mr. Rehme's question (a good guy BTW) I was stymied and fled into my next project, *Cloak & Dagger*, with me writing and Richard directing, but you can't avoid success any more than you can failure if you aspire to create something. Success has to truly dwell within you.

I've always been blessed with a love of the process of writing and later, after *Fright Night*, with directing. I think you have to love the work more than the result. Otherwise, you're a whore to your ambition and bound to be unhappy in your Hollywood career. For me anyway, the satisfaction has to come from the writing itself, and not just from the reception. If the audience loves your story and the movie that comes from it, great, but if they don't and you enjoyed writing it, you've won. There are so many reasons that a movie can fail. It can be terrific, but it misses the gestalt (witness *Thinner* which I adapted and directed and thought was terrific, but the audience didn't, nor the critics).

Also, time passes and in some cases catches up with you. Once again, check out *Thinner*. Or *Psycho II*. It was loved when it came out, a huge financial and critical success, that then was promptly forgotten for decades. It was only when mad fan Rob Galluzzo showed up on my doorstep 14 years ago to interview me for a doc that became *The Psycho Legacy* that I realized it wasn't totally forgotten. Thanks, Rob, because in my mind that began the revival of a movie that I have always been very proud of. Thank you also, to Anthony Cipriano, for writing such a wonderful afterword, and for seeing the true value in what we created way back when, and extending the *Psycho* legacy so beautifully, with *Bates Motel.*

So, what does all this mean? That even when you think you have failed or succeeded and been forgotten there is always the chance that people will remember what you have done and revive it. That happened to me this past summer when the fortieth anniversary of *Psycho II* became a huge celebration of the work that everyone had done on the movie now so long ago. I'm doing this because I was so moved by the reception and the arrival of Richard's memoirs that I didn't even know he had written, even as he was dying.

It brings tears to my eyes. It's because of all of you who are reading this now. You, the people, the audience, the fans, those who viewed the movie and found it to be the experience that I had when I was writing it and going through production. It's you, the audience, the moviegoers, the TV watchers, those who hope that movies will involve and move them when they watch it.

It's you I want to thank because it makes me feel that somehow this has all been worth it.

God bless you all.

Afterword
by Anthony S. Cipriano

Success leaves clues. And footprints. In the case of Alfred Hitchcock, giant, crater-sized footprints. Nowhere in Hitch's catalogue of films is that more evident than *Psycho*. From the day of its release, June 16, 1960, movies and the world were forever changed. Sorry *Jaws*, but I would argue it was the first summer blockbuster.

Decades pass, generations change, and yet the public continues to return to that Victorian on a hill overlooking the motel at its feet. In some kind of sick, Freudian wet dream, *Psycho* has become a gothic touchstone for the collective consciousness. By some accounts, it is the greatest film ever. So, the idea that anyone would make a sequel is... well... *psycho.*

And yet, Richard Franklin set out to do just that. Well, not just that. *Psycho II* is not your run of the mill sequel. It is something better, a legacy sequel. One that was neither lazy nor content with just refashioning the beats of the original movie for a modern-day audience. No, Richard, fresh off the success of *Road Games*, wanted a film that pushed the Norman Bates narrative forward. He wanted to... say... grab a *SHOVEL* and dig deeper. We are blessed that his cooconspirator in this endeavor was soon to be horror titan, Tom Holland. And the rest as they say is history.

Tom's book does a brilliant job detailing all the guts and glory of how the film went from idea to script to shoot to screen to hit. Clearly, I'm a fan of Tom's, but more importantly, as a writer, I am indebted to him. See, without *Psycho II*, there would be no *Bates Motel*.

My entrance into the *Psycho*-verse began back in 2004. I was a fledgling writer with my first film *12 and Holding* about to be made. *12* was my calling card back then. I think I met with almost every producer in Hollywood after that script hit the town. In every meeting, the question was, so what are you writing now? Still a mostly unknown transplant from Massachusetts, I was asking myself the same question. There was one idea I had. One that never left me, an origin story for Norman Bates. See, back in 1989, while on a family vacation, we visited Universal Studios. The Bates set was dressed because they were filming *Psycho IV*, which if you remember was one part origin story. Having just watched the trilogy and being completely obsessed with the franchise, my 13-year-old self couldn't wait to see the movie. When I did, I remember wishing there was more time for the story to unfold. How can you get to the core of a maniac in two hours? Flash forward 15 years, and

I find myself having just taken a meeting on the Universal lot and thinking, how about a *Psycho* TV series? Why not? *Smallville* worked for Superman. Why not an origin series for a villain? And so, it began. There was just one little problem. How to do it? How do you keep an audience invested in a multi-season TV series about the makings of a mass murderer? Well, lucky for me, success leaves clues.

I knew that when I was first pitching *Bates Motel* as a series, I'd need to find a way for the audience to sympathize with Norman. Since "Mother" in series would ultimately not be evil, it would have to rest on Norman's tug-of-war with sanity. I.E., Norman's character arc of *Psycho II*. Tom's script did a brilliant job of dramatizing Norman's struggle. Anthony Perkins' nuanced performance sealed it. Every time Perkins came on screen, he was simultaneously sympathetic, unnerving, and mysterious. As I was pitching the pilot for *Bates Motel*, that element plus the attack and rape on MOTHER captivated every room I pitched. It is what led to me being able to write the original pilot. I owe Tom a debt of gratitude for his guidance... (even though he wouldn't know he gave it to me until years later.) So let me take this time right now, Tom, and say thank you.

It makes me happy to see *Psycho II* enjoying this recent resurgence in popular culture. It's a rare horror sequel like *The Exorcist III* that doesn't try to compete with the original but rather breaks new ground by transcending it. The franchise is all the better for it. I have no doubt that Hitchcock and more importantly "Mother" would approve.

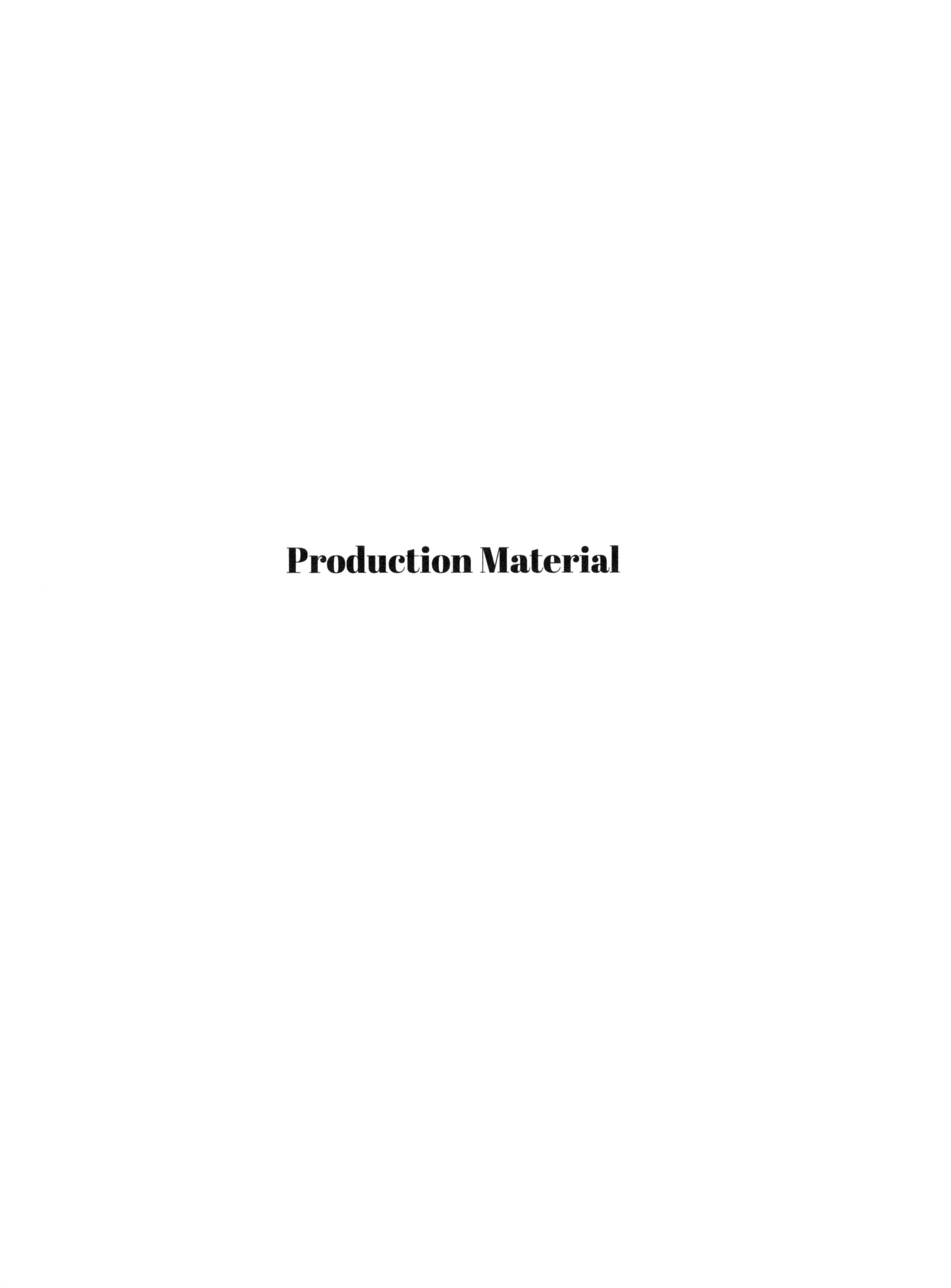

Production Material

Building the Story

Here are a selection of Tom Holland and Richard Franklin's index cards, from which the story for *Psycho II* derived…

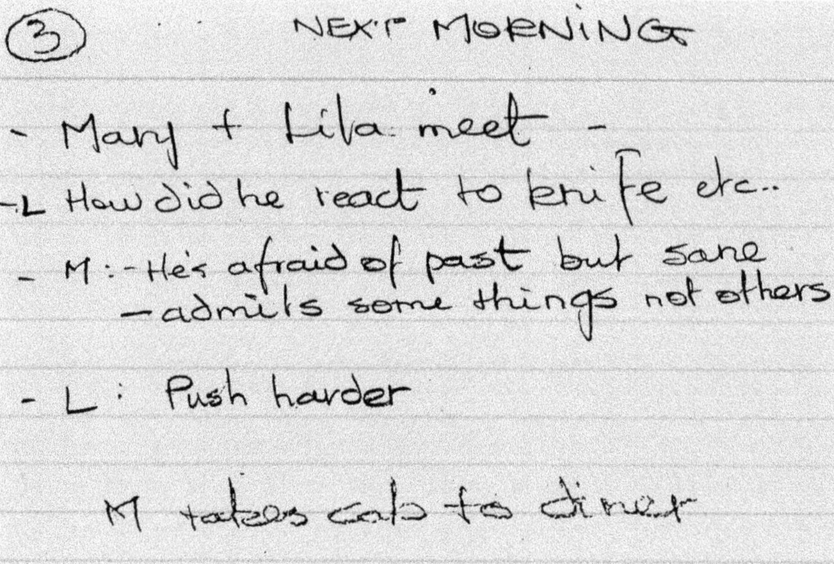

③ NEXT MORNING

- Mary + Lila meet -
- L How did he react to knife etc...
- M :- He's afraid of past but sane
  — admits some things not others

- L : Push harder

  M takes cab to diner

④A
Mary impressed N's
strength of will

④
DINER :

- Note on wheel

  Norman cracks publicly.

✶ BUT RESTRAINS
         SELF

(5)   BAR

~~Fortuitously~~ Toomey into
Hotel Bar

~~Lila~~ can't resist pumping
him ∴ jeapardising Mary

---

(6)   *

Mary talks to Lila
about diner – N's strength
– Lila reveals talked to
Toomey   (DISTURBO)

– Mary annoyed Lila
overstepping – jeopardising
– ~~dislikes Toomey~~ .... her
– Lila apologises – M agrees to go on

---

(7)

Plan ——Tea + shower

Surface * M comes to console N
     offers to stay N or M
After shower
   'Are you all right'
       ambivalent
* Cs Mary ~~bemused~~ enigmatic
     triumph't console

(8)

TOOMEY
~~DIES~~

---

(9)   *   ~~#E~~ · rest of week
- Mary begins to like **N**
- **N** resigns from diner   Raymond
- ? L gets Statler to ring ~~Rich~~
- L pressures M

~~— M finally agrees to dress up~~
~~as last attempt~~

---

(10)
- Mary finds hole (... Lila
  may be right)

- Mary's real character
  hinted at in R scene

(11) *

- while R meets sheriff
- * M tell L about hole
  L overjoyed talks
  her into dressing up
  and room

(12)   SHERIFF

- discovers Mary + Lila
  seen in car near Gorman
- Lila in bar asking Toomey
  about girl
- Lila talking Statler etc.

PSYCHO II

1. * shower murder
2. – court
    – arrival
    * flashback – note 1
    – diner I
    – Mary carpark, motel
26 + knife scene
    – night – M's bedroom
35 – morning   note 2
    + Juror II – note 3
40 + the fight
    – bar
    – kitchen – M arrives
45 + shower
52 ● T's death
    + R arrival
    + eye at wall
    + M Mary
      sheriff R
61 + N sees ghost
    – m's room furnished, note 4
65 ● Josh. Kim murder
    M finds N
    Sheriff investigates, N collapses
    + Lila surprises M
    + blood in bathroom
    – eye watches M
    – M realises L
      voice speaks to N
    – N stands guard
    – phonecall 2
    – R talks N – N talks of real mother
    – M, L argue
    + exhumation
      phonecall 3 – N starts to slip
    – R follows L
      swamp scene
    ● L's death
    + R into house – N surprises

Richard Franklin's Script Plotting Notes

Storyboard and
Screenplay Excerpts

#02149   2
                                              Rev. 6/28/82

C   EXT. BATES' HOUSE - NIGHT - FOOTAGE FROM <u>PSYCHO I</u>   C

        Rising high above the motel on a rise, staring down at the
        wood structure, dwarfing it. The Victorian house is well
        kept up, but antiquated, brooding, somehow threatening. In
        one bedroom window a light shines, and in that window sits
        the figure of Mrs. Bates in her chair, as though watching
        over the business of the motel below. The sound of Norman's
        fearful, shocked voice shatters the night.

                        NORMAN'S VOICE
                Mother! Oh, God, what...blood,
                blood...mother!

        And the night closes over the house, swallowing it in
        blackness until we:

                                        MATCH DISSOLVE TO

1   EXT. BATES' MOTEL AND HOUSE - DAWN (TITLES ROLL)   1

        Slowly the sun bleeds in over the house and motel, and we
        suddenly realize we are seeing new color footage. Time has
        passed, many years, for now both structures show the wear of
        years, the signs of neglect, broken shingles, flecked paint,
        lopsided blinds. But they are both still there, the Bates'
        house and motel. And still habitable.

MATTE

SC. 4   NORMAN AND RICHMOND ARRIVE

X'e should be a little more Right
cat can come from bottom Right.

---

4   EXT. BATES' MOTEL AND HOUSE - DAY   4

        A Mercedes drives past the shabby motel and stops before the
        steps leading up to the large Victorian house.

5   OMITTED   5

6   EXT. STAIRS - DAY   6

        As Norman emerges from the passenger side of the car, he
        stops and takes in the old house which he hasn't seen for
        years. The Doctor follows his gaze.

                              DR. RICHMOND
                    Well, home sweet home.

                              NORMAN
                    Yes.

        His gaze travels from the house to an old Buick parked
        adjacent to the motel office. Dr. Richmond follows his gaze
        once more.

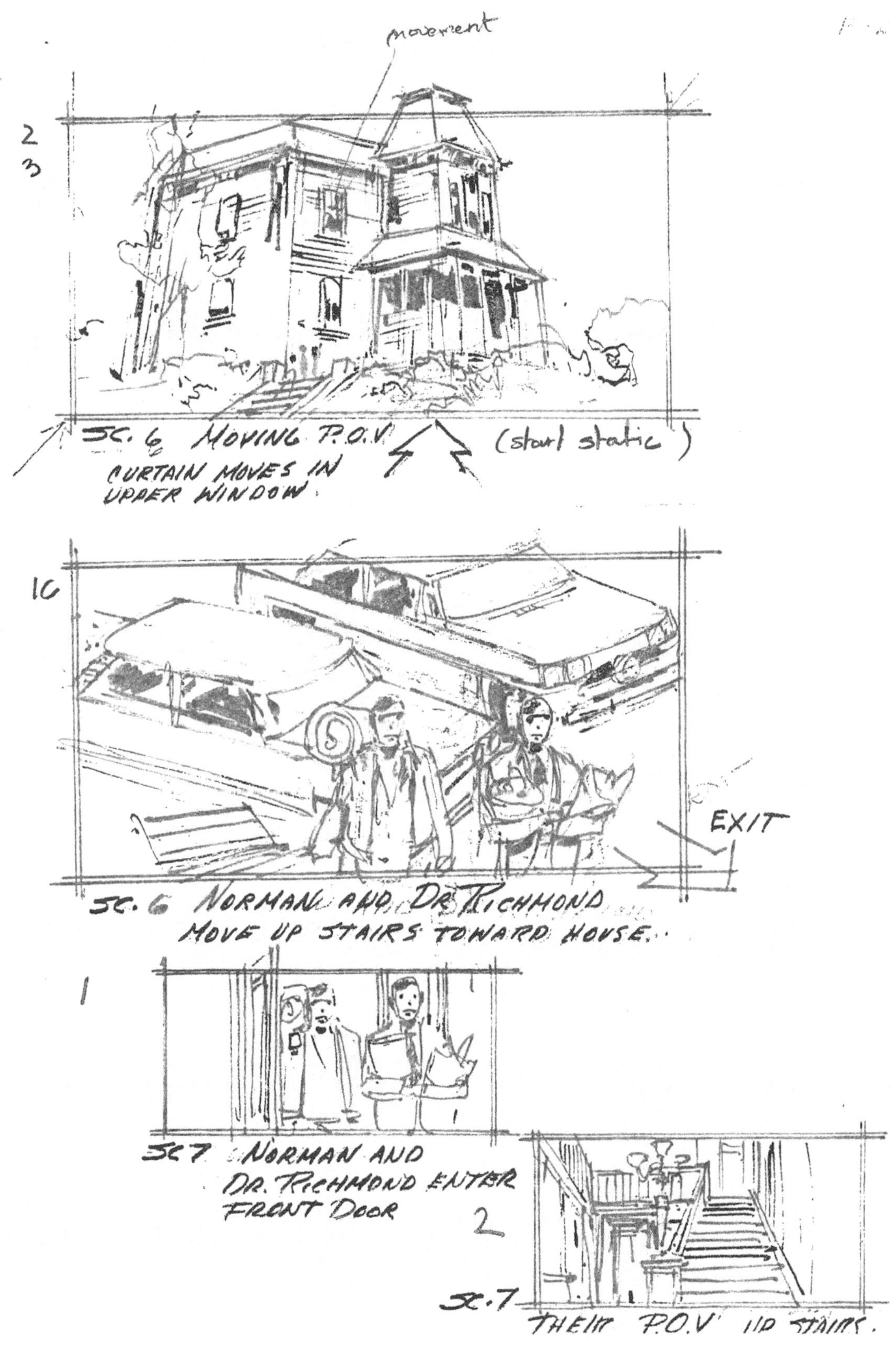

movement
2
3
SC. 6   MOVING P.O.V   (start static)
CURTAIN MOVES IN
UPPER WINDOW
10
EXIT
SC. 6   NORMAN AND DR. RICHMOND
MOVE UP STAIRS TOWARD HOUSE.
1
SC 7   NORMAN AND
DR. RICHMOND ENTER
FRONT DOOR
2
SC. 7   THEIR P.O.V UP STAIRS.

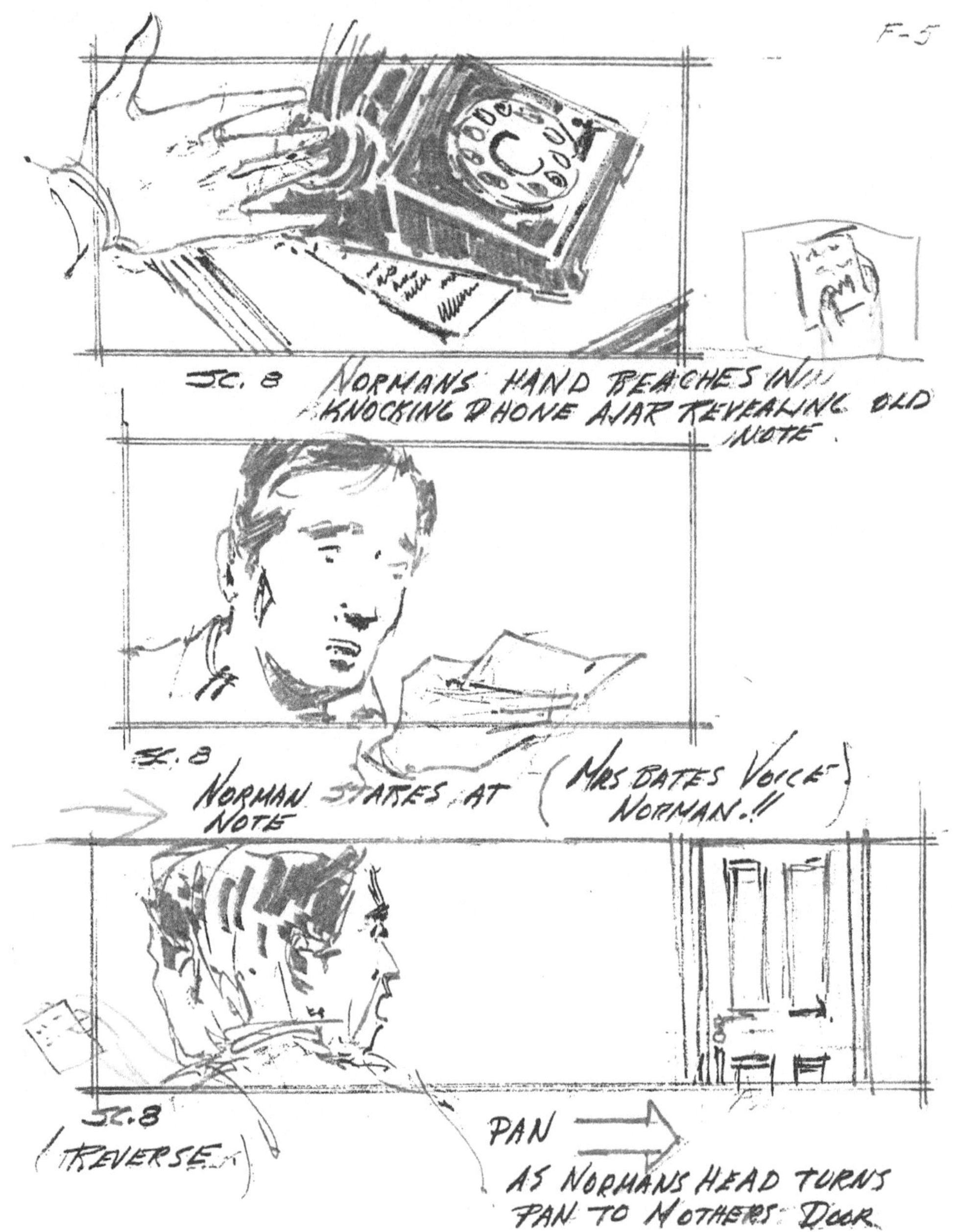

8 INT. SECOND FLOOR LANDING - DAY 8

Just as he reaches the landing and is about to turn right to his old room, he glances to his left and sees the old black phone sitting there on a small table. Picking up the phone to check the dial tone, he knocks it ajar. Beneath the phone, a yellowed sheet of paper protrudes. He picks up the slip of paper. It is an old note written in pencil. It reads, "Norman, I'll be home late, fix your own dinner, love, M." He stiffens, the paper slipping from his numb fingers, his gaze rising to the door further along the balcony. It is old and cracked, beaten by time, scratched by misuse. Suddenly he hears a voice echoing inside his own head.

    MRS. BATES' VOICE

Norman!

SC. 16 NORMAN AND MARY LEAVE DINNER
MAGIC HOUR (ROMANTIC WITH PART OF BEHIND STORM)

- perhaps there should be a small cross road - maybe a gas station beyond diner.

- more cars in fg carpark

- a little more hilly

#02149   16

16   EXT. DINER - NIGHT   16

        The diner is lit, customers still eating, people inside
        still working. Norman comes out the front door, dressed to
        go home, off work at last. As he winds his way through the
        parking lot, he notices Mary Samuels behind him talking on a
        pay phone on the wall of the diner. Her voice rises with
        anger as she talks, dragging him to a halt.

17 NIGHT NORMAN AND MARY WALK TO MOTEL OFFICE
JC. 18 NORMAN AND MARY ENTER MOTEL OFFICE RAINING OUTSIDE
PAN
JC. 18 NORMAN REACHES FOR KEY.

17   CONTINUED   17

        A high-pitched scream of feminine pleasure echoes out of one
        of the rooms followed by a roar of masculine laughter.
        Norman throws a nervous glance down the veranda toward the
        room. The sounds are muted by the patter of rain, but they
        have that musty forced patina of false pleasure, the kind men
        quite often pay for. When Norman turns back to Mary, he is
        embarrassed. She, too, finds it difficult to meet his gaze.
        He quickly moves her down the verandah, away from the room,
        toward the motel office.

                            NORMAN
                Come on, I'll get a room key for you.

18   INT. MOTEL OFFICE - NIGHT   18

        The rain beats a heavier tattoo on the roof as the two of
        them enter. Norman peers through the open doorway behind
        the counter into the parlor. From the slovenly mess within,
        he can tell it's obviously Mr. Toomey's living quarters.

                            NORMAN
                Mr. Toomey?

        No answer. Norman walks behind the counter to the keyboard
        where all the room keys hang. Two are missing. His hand
        pauses above the key to room #1, then shifts to #6. He takes
        it down from the board and turns to Mary.

        A feminine scream of pleasure echoes into the office from a
        motel room out on the verandah. His gaze shifts to the open
        door onto the verandah, then back to Mary.

                            NORMAN
                      (with a
                      forced smile)
                Why don't you wait here while I
                check the room. Just to make sure
                the linen's fresh.

        He slips out the door onto the verandah without giving her a
        chance to reply. She stares about the office. It's worse
        than neglected and threadbare; somehow it's cheap and
        sleazy, as though Mr. Toomey has permanently left his mark
        there. The sound of rain falling begins to slacken. The
        fat man suddenly shoulders his way through the door from the
        outside behind Mary, catching her staring about the room.

                            MR. TOOMEY
                Thinking about stealing something?

                                              CONTINUED

NORMAN HEARS TAPPING LOOKS OFF

SHADOWY FIGURE MOVES PAST WINDOW.

66   CONTINUED   66

3   The tapping drags him out from under the veranda in the
    direction of the steps leading up to the house. He glances
    about' nothing. He is about to return to his painting when
    the tapping comes again.

                              4 POV
    He looks up at the house, and [there, in the bedroom window,
    stands his mother, a huge figure draped in dark billowing
    clothes, outlined in shadows, smudged by the distance. He
    drops his brush and stares up in horror.

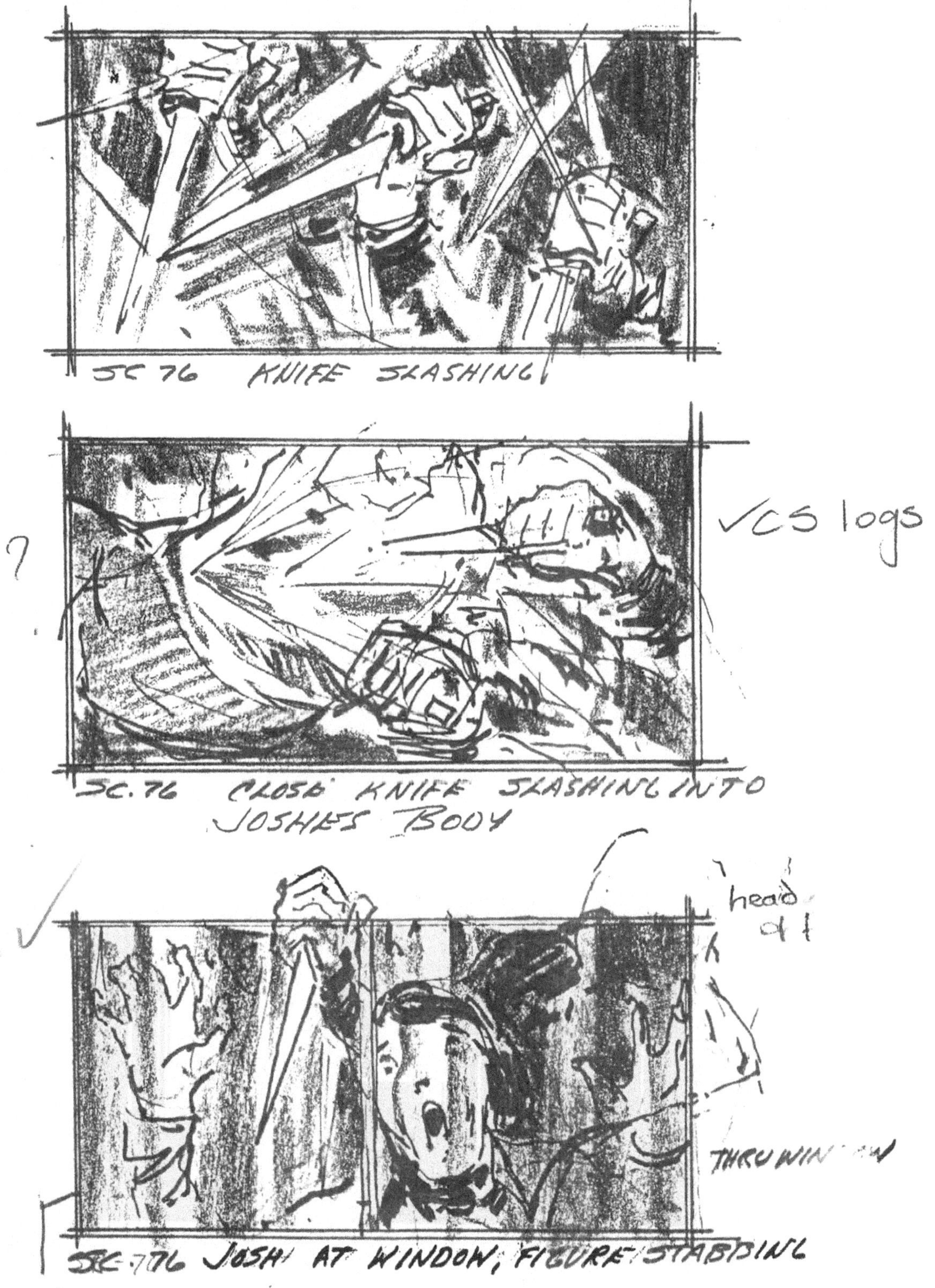

SC.76   KNIFE SLASHING
?
✓CS logs
SC.76   CLOSE KNIFE SLASHING INTO
JOSHES BODY
head
✓
THRU WINDOW
SC.76 JOSH AT WINDOW, FIGURE STABBING

76   EXT. HOUSE - GROUND LEVEL WINDOW - DAY   76

Through the filth of the dirty window, Kim sees the blurred
figure of Mrs. Bates bearing down on her boyfriend. Josh
leaps to his feet, his damaged fingers fumbling to undo the
window catch. Mrs. Bates, an enormous mass of black
clothing, rears up behind him. The knife glints in the sun-
light pouring through the window. The blade flashes down at
the boy's exposed back. Kim screams.

And it falls again and again and again, plunging into Josh
while Kim screams, an unending cacaphony as she stares trans-
fixed at the bloody ballet within, obscured from clear
vision by the filth of the window.

The boy's dying fingertips reach out for the glass, for
freedom, for safety, but it's too late. As they slowly
slide down from the glass, they leave streaks of comparative
cleanliness behind, bars of light that Kim can see through
more clearly. And then the fingertips are gone, sinking out
of sight as the boy falls to the floor below. Within, Kim
can see the striated image of Mrs. Bates bent over her victim,
her gore-drenched blade momentarily still. Then the huge
woman slowly shifts her bulk, her attention turning to Kim. eyes!

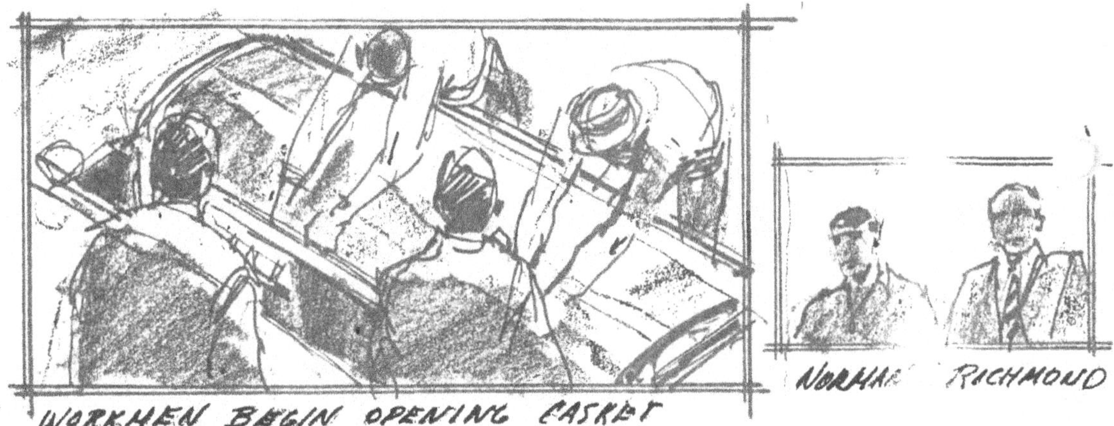

117   EXT. CEMETERY - DAY (SAME)   117
                                                           (X)
Near the road the cemetery Sexton and Deputy Norris stand
talking. The police officer hands the Sexton a printed form.

                    SEXTON
          I don't see what all the rush was ---

                    DEPUTY
          Sheriff's orders ---

And beyond them, in the middle of a row of graves, Norman
and Dr. Richmond walk up to an open gravesight. A coffin
is lifted from the grave and its lid pried back. The   (X)
sunny day seems incongrous with the setting. The two
men peer into the remains within the coffin.

The mummified remains of Mrs. Bates stares back at them.
The skin is shriveled and brown, pulled away from the mouth
revealing a skeleton's smile. The eyes are gone, just empty
sockets peering up. The bridge of the nose has collapsed,
the hair dry and wild, the cheeks sunken. The corpse is
dressed in the mouldering remains of a high-necked, old-
fashioned dress. Norman jerks away in revulsion (per Tsbody)

                    DR. RICHMOND
          Believe me now?

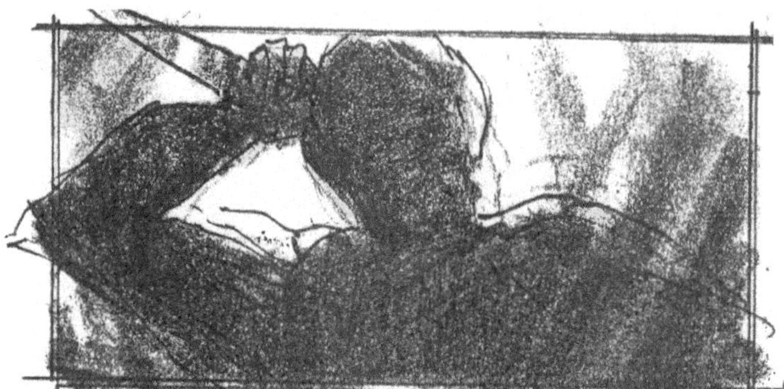

SC. 137 SHADOWY FIGURE SLASHES
WITH KNIFE

SC. 137 KNIFE PLUNGES INTO MOUTH

SC. 137. KNIFE BLADE EMERGING
FROM BACK OF NECK.

Behind her, a massive shadow suddenly detaches itself from
the deeper darkness of the basement. It moves forward
rapidly, silently, advancing on Lila's turned back. All
that is seen of it in the dimness is the hem of a cheap
cotton print dress, and the black, androgenous orthopedic
shoes beneath. A blade gleams in the scarce light as the
huge shadow raises a butcher knife high in the air. At that
moment, Lila senses something, perhaps hears the wheeze of
leathery ancient lungs. She whirls just as the butcher
knife flashes down. She opens her mouth to scream, and the
blade slices between her teeth, and down, burying itself in
her throat, piercing the back of her neck, the blade pro-
truding a good five inches into the air.

NOTE: THIS MATERIAL IS <u>CONFIDENTIAL</u> AND WILL BE DISTRIBUTED

TO CAST AND CREW DURING PRODUCTION.   PLEASE <u>DO</u> <u>NOT</u>

ATTACH TO SCRIPT.

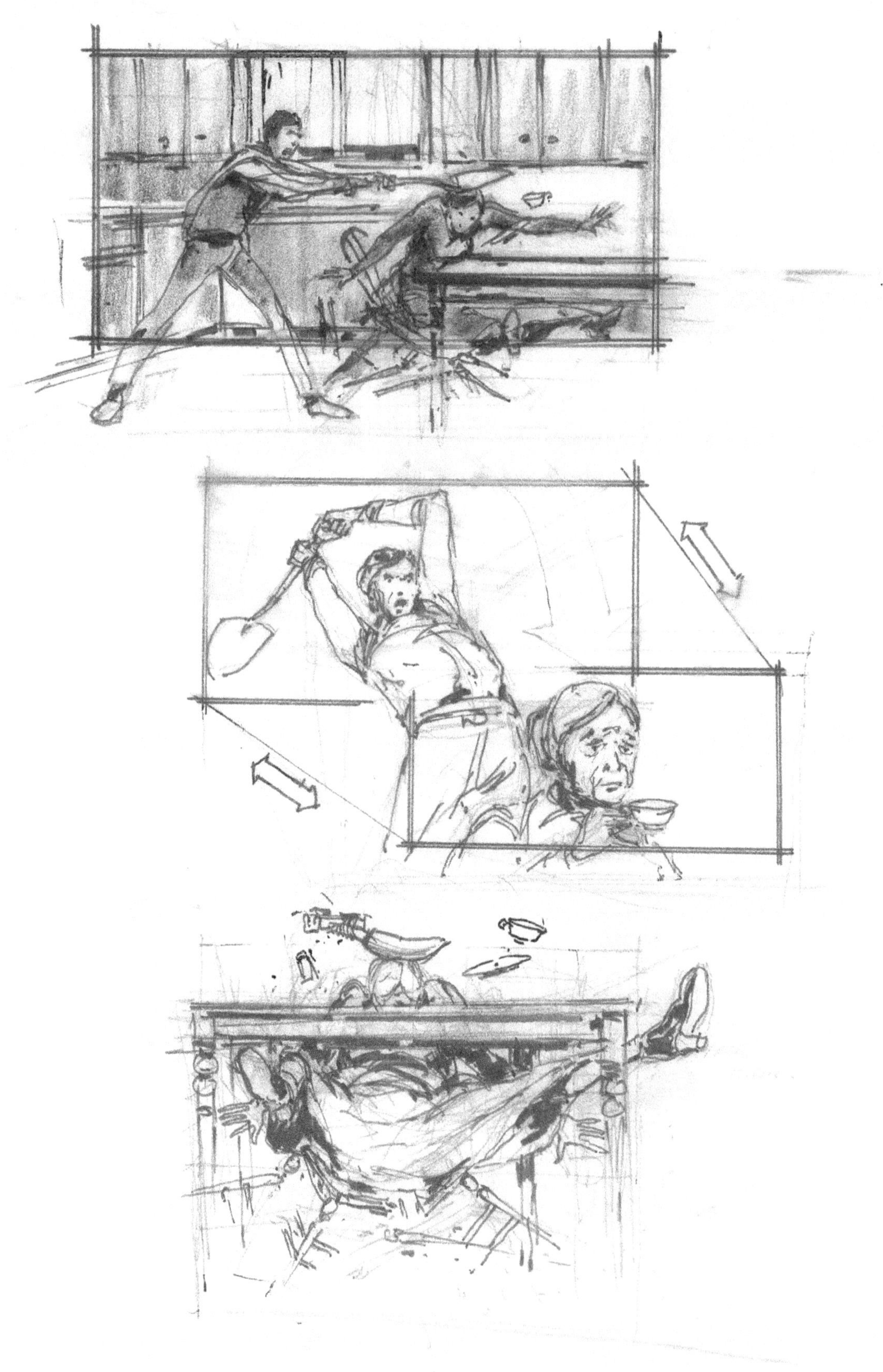

   CONTINUED - 2

                              NORMAN
          Yes.

She picks up the cup of tea and is about to drink, but
hesitates, cup poised.

                            MRS. SPOOL
          By the time I got out, you'd already
          had your 'troubles' and been committed.
          I decided to wait for you, and then
          when I saw what they were doing to
          my poor little boy, I couldn't stand
          it. After all, you're all I have
          in this world.

She takes a sip of tea.

                              NORMAN
          Thank you, mother.

Without a sound he steps from the kitchen sink, picks up
the shovel in the corner and swings it high over his head
in an arc, bringing the heavy spaded end smashing down on
the back of her skull.

The force of the blow snaps vertebrae from the top of her
neck to the small of her back, collapsing the legs of the
chair beneath her, the first tier, then the second, driving
her and the seat to the floor in an explosion of broken
wood, shattered flesh and bone and dancing dust motes.

NORMAN

"The backstairs, maybe they went down that way."

After Lila's death, as Mary backs away from him on the phone.

He says: "Do I have to kill her?"
Then: "Oh, mother, please don't _make_ me."

Talking on the phone as Mary comes up the stairs dressed as
his mother:

"But mother, you don't understand about Mary. She'd never hurt
me. She cares about me too much --
                         (pause as he listens to the
                          voice on the other end, the
                          one in reality in his head)
I know you care more, mother --

"Mother how can you think such a thing?
I could never do anything like _that_.
(Especially not to someone I care about.)"

Shooting Schedule

CAMERA AND DATE	DESCRIPTION OF SET OR LOCATION	ACTORS WORKING	SEQ	PAGE	VEHICLES LIVESTOCK PROPS	DAY OR NITE
22nd Day Friday 7/30/82 STAGE 24	INT. SECOND FLOOR LANDING Sc. 126 Mary on extension trying to get Norman to hand up.	2 MARY 1 NORMAN (V.O.)		5/8		D
	INT. SECOND FLOOR BALCONY Sc. 156 pt. Mary on phone -- Dr. Raymond out of rear hall -- She stabs him -- over the rail.	2 MARY (AS MOTHER) 3 DR. RAYMOND ATMOS: St. Dbl. Raymond		1- 1/8	SPEC. EFX: KNIFE INTO CHEST	D
	INT. PORTICO/STAIRS/ BALCONY Sc. 156 pt. Raymond falls to floor/ splat.	2 MARY (AS MOTHER) 3 RAYMOND ATMOS: St. Dbl. Raymond		2/8	DUMMY BODY TO MATCH SPEC. EFX: KNIFE PLUNGES THROUGH BODY - BOUNCE OFF RAILING SPEC. NOTE: AIR BAG? CAMERA: 3 CAMERAS FOR FALL	D
	END OF TWENTY-SECOND DAY	TOTAL PAGES: 2				

CAMERA AND DATE	DESCRIPTION OF SET OR LOCATION	ACTORS WORKING	SEQ	PAGE	VEHICLES LIVESTOCK PROPS	DAY OR NITE
16th Day Thursday 7/22/82 STAGE 24	INT. BASEMENT Sc. 137 Lila gets it.	4 LILA Mother (Feet and Arm)		4/8	MOTHER'S COSTUME BREAD KNIFE BUTCHER KNIFE SPEC. EFX: SLAB MOVES KNIFE INTO MOUTH AND OUT BACK OF THROAT AND BLOOD SPEC. NOTE: FURNITURE -- DOLLY FOR LILA'S SCRAMBLE	D
	INT. BASEMENT AND FRUIT CELLAR Scs. 141, 142, 143 Dr. Raymond surprised to meet Norman in the basement.	1 NORMAN 3 DR. RAYMOND		2-1/8	SPEC. EFX: FLOOR SLAB ROCKS WHEN RAYMOND STEPS ON IT DOOR CLOSES	D
	END OF SIXTEENTH DAY	TOTAL PAGES: 2-5/8				

CAMERA AND DATE	DESCRIPTION OF SET OR LOCATION	ACTORS WORKING	SEQ	PAGE	VEHICLES LIVESTOCK PROPS	DAY OR NITE
2nd Day 7/1/82 (Cont'd) BACKLOT	EXT. HOUSE AND MOTEL Sc. 61 Mary comes out and finds Norman with paint and Dr. Raymond -- she gets a ride.	1 NORMAN 2 MARY 3 DR. RAYMOND		1-6/8	PAINT AS BEFORE DR. RAYMOND'S MERCEDES SPEC. NOTE: MOTEL ONE-QUARTER PAINTED	D
	EXT. HOUSE AND MOTEL Sc. 62 pt. Plate for Mercedes drive-away from house (Norman painting in b.g.)	1 NORMAN		1/8	SPEC. NOTE: LONG DOLLY SHOT MOTEL ONE-QUARTER PAINTED	D
	EXT. HOUSE AND MOTEL Sc. 55 Pan from Norman in window to Toomey packing in motel office.	5 TOOMEY ATMOS: Dbl. Norman (Face In Window)		2/8	SUITCASE TOOMEY'S CAR	N
	POINT OF VIEW FROM HOUSE WINDOW TO MOTEL Scs. 51, 52 pt. Over Norman's shoulder down to motel and Toomey by car, into motel -- lights on.	5 TOOMEY ATMOS: Dbl. Norman's Hand On Drapes		2/8	TOOMEY'S CAR SPEC. NOTE: LIGHTS GO ON IN MOTEL	N
	END OF SECOND DAY	TOTAL PAGES: 5-4/8				

SHOOTING SCHEDULE

PROD. NO. 02149		June 28, 1982
-LE PSYCHO II		**DIRECTOR** RICHARD FRANKLIN
START 6/30/82		**ASST. DIR.** DON ZEPFEL
CLOSE 8/9/82	**CAMERA DAYS** 28 + Stock	**UNIT MGR.** BILL GRAY

CAMERA DAY AND DATE	DESCRIPTION OF SET OR LOCATION	ACTORS WORKING	SEQ	PAGE	VEHICLES LIVESTOCK PROPS	DAY OR NITE
1st Day Wednesday 6/30/82 STAGE 34	INT. COURTROOM Sc. 3 Norman is judged restored to sanity and set free. *TRAILER SHOT*	1 NORMAN 3 DR. RAYMOND 4 LILA 16 DA 18 JUDGE 20 DEPUTY PUBLIC DEFENDER 21 BAILIFF ATMOS: 1 Stenographer 1 Court Clerk 2 Lawyers 1 Deputy Sheriff 1 New Defendant 12 Spectators and Witnesses	2-	6/8	STENO MACHINE (SEG) BRIEFCASES DOCUMENTS GAVEL PETITION SPEC. NOTE: TRIAL OF NEW DEFENDANT CONTINUES IN B.G. OF SC. 3-A (HALLWAY)	D
	INT. HALL BY COURTROOM Sc. 3-A Lila confronts Norman in hall.	1 NORMAN 3 DR. RAYMOND 4 LILA ATMOS: 2 Lawyers (New) 3 Spectators 18 Atmos. As Before		1	PAY PHONES SPEC. NOTE: TRIAL CROWD VISIBLE THROUGH COURT DOOR IN B.G.	D
COURT-HOUSE SQUARE	EXT. HOTEL AND STREET Scs. 131, 132 Lila drives off -- Raymond follows.	3 DR. RAYMOND 4 LILA ATMOS: 13 Street Atmos. 5 Drivers 2 Kids On Bikes		2/8	BIKES LILA'S CAR RAYMOND'S MERCEDES 10 ND CARS (SEG)	D
	INT. DR. RAYMOND'S OFFICE Sc. 53 Dr. Raymond tells Norman he will come at end of week.	3 DR. RAYMOND		2/8	PHONE	N

Post-Production
Schedule

START JUNE 20 *(20 Weeks)* *RICHARD FRANKLIN*   Dat

TITLE: *PSYCHO II*   **PROD. #** *02149*   ASPEC RATI

TO: PRODUCER: *H. GREEN*   DIRECTOR: *R. FRANKLIN*
PROJECT EXEC: *N. Tanen*   EDITOR: *A. London*

...IES: N. Tanen/T. Mount/V. Fields/J. Christian/P. Wilson

FROM: Phil Scott
(TARGET DATES)

☐ US & CANADA   ☐ FOREIGN
☒ WORLDWIDE   ☐ DISCO'V
☐ NETWORK   ☐ PAY TV

BASED ☒ Budget
ON: ☐ Sales Print Require

Target Date	Task
AUG 10	FINISH SHOOTING *5.6 wk* (Principal Photography) — SOUND EDITOR: *J. STACY* — LOOP EDITOR: *G. HUDSON*
AUG 24	FINISH EDITOR'S ASSEMBLAGE (1st Cut) / LEGAL: Start work on Main and End Title Copy
	EDITOR: Order opticals and titles as soon as possible to allow time for remakes
OCT 5	FINISH EDITING OF "DIRECTOR'S CUT" (*6* weeks)
	NOTE: Director's cut should be finished by this date, to allow time for Post-personnel to complete their work satisfactorily to the Director and Pro incurring costly premium time to meet the Dubbing Date.
OCT 12	FINISH TEMP DUBB, TANEN/MOUNT SCREENING AND RECUTS BEFORE
?	RECRUITED-AUDIENCE (TEST) SCREENING
OCT 18	START POST-PRODUCTION WORK---Preparation for Dubbing (Turn over B&W Dupes to Music, Sound Effects and Looping)
OCT 20	DELIVER FINAL MAIN AND END TITLE COPY to Producer, Direct Project Executive and others concerned for revisions or a
	NOTE: Main & End Title Copy, Concept, Design, and Optical work should be star early, as experience has proven it usually holds up sales prints if del
OCT 25 to Nov 12	LOOPING (ADR) PERIOD---Necessary looping (ADR) time shoul be scheduled between these dates.
OCT 27	ORDER MAIN AND END TITLES
NOV 3	CODE RATING SCREENING. CARA (Code and Rating Administrati requests film be sent unaccompanie
NOV 4	FINISH DELIVERY OF OPTICALS/MAIN AND END TITLE NEGATIVE.
NOV 8	TAKE KEY NUMBERS AND PICK NEGATIVE
NOV 15	CUT NEGATIVE AND MAKE YCM PROTECTIVE MASTERS
	NOTE: Opticals/Titles should be in work print before this date to avoid excessive
NOV 12	TECHNICOLOR TIMING SCREENING---Work Print run at Technico with Director, Cameraman (if available), Technicolor Time Editor to determine timing of answer print.
NOV 17	MUSIC SCORING AND DIALOGUE PRE-DUBB COMPOSER: MUSIC EDITOR:
NOV 22 to DEC 10	START DUBBING at: *UNIVERSAL ROOM 3* *15* Days
DEC 14	COMPOSITE PREVIEW (PA) PRINT (Partially or fully correc

Post-Production
Budget

A/C 851 EDITING AND PROJECTION

SUB DESCRIPTION	MEN	WKS.	RATE	AMOUNT	TOTAL
1 FILM EDITOR ANDREW LONDON					
ACCUM. TO					
(SHOOTING PERIOD) 5.6 WEEKS					
DIST LOC.					
STUDIO	1	5.60	1,300		7,280
(EDITING) 9 WEEKS					
FINISH EDITOR"S ASSEMBLY	1	2.CO	1,300		2,600
DIRECTOR"S CUT	1	6.CO	1,300		7,800
TEMP. DUBB,WP SCRN.,EXC CHANGE	1	1.CO	1,300		1,300
(DUBBING PREPARATION) 5 WEEKS	1	5.CO	1,300		6,500
(DUBBING) 3 WEEKS	1	3.00	1,300		3,900
(PREVIEWS) 1 WEEK	1	1.00	1,300		1,300
(POST PREVIEW PERIOD) 2 WEEKS					
AFTER PREV. EDITING - PIC. CHANGES	1	1.00	1,300		1,300
RECUTS M,E,D,&N-REMAKE O,T,&RE-DUBB	1	1.00	1,300		1,300
CHECK & APPROVE FINAL ANSWER PRINT					
WEEKEND WORK PROVISION DAYS					
FILM EDITOR TOTAL 25.6 WEEKS					33,280
2 ASSISTANT FILM EDITOR					
ACCUM. TO					
(SHOOTING PERIOD)					
DISTANT LOCATIONS					
STUDIO	1	5.60	765		4,284
(EDITING)	1	9.00	765		6,885
(DUBBING PREPARATION)	1	5.00	765		3,825
(DUBBING)	1	3.00	765		2,295
(PREVIEW)	1	1.00	765		765
(POST-PREVIEW)	1	2.00	765		1,530
(CLEAN UP PERIOD)	1	1.00	765		765
OVERTIME PROVISION					
WEEKEND WORK PROV. DAYS					
ASSISTANT EDITOR TOTAL 26.6 WEEKS					20,349
3 NEGATIVE CUTTING					
1ST CUT	RLS	1	10.00	400	4,000
RECUT	RLS	1	8.00	200	1,600
SYNC TRACKS	RLS.	1	18.00	27	486

NEGATIVE CUTTING TOTAL					6,086
4 APPRENTICE FILM EDITORS					
ACCUM. TO					
(SHOOTING PERIOD)					
DISTANT LOCATIONS					
STUDIO					
(EDITING)					
(DUBBING PREPARATION)					
(DUBBING)					
(PREVIEW)					
(POST-PREVIEW)					

PSYCHO II   BUDGET   JUN 11,1982   4:32PM   PAGE 34
   (CLEAN UP PERIOD)
   OVERTIME PROVISION
   WEEKEND WORK PROV.   DAYS

     APPRENT. EDITORS TOTAL   WEEKS ....

5 PROJECTIONISTS
    DISTANT LOCATIONS
    STUDIO   1   10.00   560   5,600
                                    ----   -----   ----   -----
     PROJECTIONISTS TOTAL   5,600

6 MISCELLANEOUS EDITORIAL SERVICE ALLOW.   1   20.00   190   3,800

7 SOUND EFFECTS EDITING
    PREP & CREATIVE SPEC. EFX. (2 MEN)
    SOUND EFX. & PROD. DIALOGUE EDIT. (5 MEN) 1   8.00   5,190   41,520
    POST-DUPING CHANGES PROV. (5 MEN)   1   2.40   5,190   12,456
    WEEKEND WORK PROV.   DA   1   8.00   2,076   16,608
    OVERTIME PROVISION

     SOUND EDITORS TOTAL   70,584

8 SOUND EFX. & ADR DIAL. EDITING CREW   1   1.00   6,966   6,966

9 ADR (LOOP) DIALOGUE EDITING   1   8.00   1,776   14,208
    POST-DUPING CHANGES PROV.   1   2.40   1,776   4,262
    WEEKEND WORK PROVISION.   1   4.00   710   2,840
    OVERTIME PROVISION.

     ADR DIAL. EDITING TOTAL   21,310

30 TVL & L.E.

34 CONTINUITY EXP.
    PREPARATION   1   10.00   70   700
    SUPPLIES & DUPLICATING   270   270
                                                        ---- ----
     CONT. EXPENSE TOTAL   970

51 PURCHASES   1,500 1,500

56 ROOM & EQUIP. RENTAL   Use Universal KEM

60 MISC. EXP.   200   200
                                                        ---- ----

A/C 851 EDITING & PROJ. TOTAL   170,645

A/C 853 MUSIC

SUB DESCRIPTION	MEN	HRS.	RATE	AMOUNT	TOTAL
1 MUSIC & SONG CLEAR., PURCH.,ROYAL.				3,000	3,000
2 SONG WRITERS SALARIES					
3 ARRANGERS				10,000	10,000
4 COPYISTS				8,500	8,500
5 COMPOSERS UNDERSCORE				20,000	20,000
MUSIC SUPERVISION					
COMP. & SUP. TOTAL					20,000
6 PRESCORE MUSICIANS					
7 UNDERSCORE MUSICIANS(40 MEN)					
MUSICIANS	12	15.00	81		14,526
MUSICIANS	10	15.00	61		9,079
MUSICIANS	33	15.00	40		19,973
CONTRACTOR	1	15.00	40		605
CONDUCTOR	1	15.00	161		2,421
UNDER. MUSIC. TOTAL					46,605
8 SYNC MEN, REH. PIANISTS & COACHES					
10 SINGERS & VOICE DBLS.					
15 MUSIC EDITORS				10,000	10,000
30 TRAVEL & LIVING EXP.					
56 RENTAL & CARTAGE				1,250	1,250
60 MISC. EXP.				6,750	6,750
A/C 853 MUSIC TOTAL					106,105

A/C 855 SOUND (POST PRODUCTION)

SUB DESCRIPTION	MEN	WKS.	RATE	AMOUNT	TOTAL
2 DUBBING					
TEMP DUBBS ALLOWANCE					
DIALOGUE PRE-DUBB					
BEFORE PREVIEW DUBB	1	3.00	8,300		24,900
AFTER PREVIEW RE-DUBB	1	.60	8,300		4,980
WEEKEND WORK PROV. DAYS					
DUBB. CREW TOTAL					29,880
3 ADR (LOOP) DIALOGUE RECORDING	1	2.00	3,800		7,600
5 PRESCORE RECORDING					
6 UNDERSCORE RECORDING	1	1.00	6,200		6,200
7 FOLEY & SOUND EFFECTS RECORDING	1	1.00	6,350		6,350
12 POST PROD. MAG FILM TRANSFERS (LABOR ONLY)	1	14.00	764		10,696
30 TRAVEL & LIVING EXP.					
51 PURCHASE & SUPPLIES				500	500
56 EQUIP. RENTAL				1,500	1,500
60 MISC. EXP.				200	200
A/C 855 SOUND(PP) TOTAL					62,926

PSYCHO II   BUDGET   JUN 11,1982   4:32PM   PAGE 37
A/C 857 FILM & STOCK SHOTS (POST PRODUCTION)

SUB DESCRIPTION		EST # FT.	RATE	AMOUNT	TOTAL
1 FILM LEADER	1	170,000	.0071		1,207
3 STOCK SHOTS-PURCHASE				1,500	1,500
4 " " -DIRECT LABOR				2,000	2,000
5 " " -FILM & PROCESSING				1,500	1,500
6 EDITOR"S PICT. REPRINTS-ONE LITE	1	7,000	.2713		1,899
EDITOR"S PICT. REPTS-SIMPLE TIM.					
EDITOR"S PICT. REPTS TOTAL					1,899
8 VIDEO CASSETTES/TAPES				500	500
9 B&W REVERSAL DUPES (9 DUPES)	1	55,800	.1339		7,472
12 MAGNETIC FILM & TAPE	1	400,000	.0230		9,200
17 OPTICAL SOUND TRACK	1	5,000	.4659		6,989
19 1ST ANSWER PRINT	1	9,300	.9984		9,285
FINAL ANSWER PRINT	1	7,000	.4000		2,800
ANSWER PRINT TOTAL					12,085
21 YCM PROTECTION MASTER	1	9,300	.8475		7,882
23 INTERNEG & CRI ALLOW.					
27 35MM STUDIO COMPOSITE REF. PRINT					
33 LAB OVERTIME PROV.				500	500
35 LAB MISC. LABOR				1,000	1,000
60 MISC. EXP.				100	100
A/C 857 FILM & STOCK SHOTS TOTAL					53,833

PSYCHO II   BUDGET   JUN 11,1982   4:32PM   PAGE 38

A/C 859 TITLES, OPTICALS, & INSERTS

SUB DESCRIPTION	MEN	DAYS	RATE	AMOUNT	TOTAL
1 MAIN & END TITLES				8,000	8,000
TITLE DESIGNER					
TITLE DESIGNER TOTAL					8,000
3 OPTICAL EFFECTS				20,000	20,000
4 INSERTS				3,000	3,000
5 TRADEMARK, ETC.				500	500
6 TITLES OTHER THAN MAIN & END					
60 MISC. EXP.				200	200
A/C 859 TITLES, OPT.&INSERTS TOTAL					31,700

A/C 861 INSURANCE

SUB DESCRIPTION	AMOUNT	TOTAL
1 CAST INSURANCE	29,200	29,200
3 NEGATIVE INSURANCE	6,800	6,800
4 OTHER INSURANCE EXTRA EXPENSE	3,500	3,500
A/C 861 INSURANCE TOTAL		39,500

A/C 863 FRINGES BENEFITS - BELOW THE LINE

SUB DESCRIPTION	AMOUNT	TOTAL
2 PROV. FOR RETO. WAGES		
3 VAC., H&W, PEN., ETC.		510,504
A/C 863 F/B TOTAL		510,504

The Preview

YOU ARE CORDIALLY INVITED TO THE CAST AND CREW SCREENING
OF "PSYCHO II" ON MONDAY, JANUARY 31ST, AT 8:00 P.M. THE
SCREENING WILL BE HELD IN THE ALFRED HITCHCOCK THEATRE,
UNIVERSAL STUDIOS.

THIS INVITATION WILL ADMIT YOU AND ONE GUEST. INVITATIONS
ARE NON-TRANSFERABLE.

PLEASE R.S.V.P.: 508-3138.

<u>GUEST LIST - "PSYCHO II" SCREENING - MON., JAN. 31ST - 8:00 P.M.</u>

<u>A</u>

Sheila Adams
Jim Alexander
Jim Allen
Bruce Andrews
Mel Arnold
Burt Astor

<u>B</u>

Dick Babin
Jerry Barton
Ron Batzdorff
Max Bell
Earl Bellamy
Lon Bender
Bruce Berman
Pam Brewer
Karl Brindle
Fred Brost
Ed Brown
Victoria Brown
Robert Alan Browne
Clyde Bryan
Claudia Bryar

<u>C</u>

Brendan Cahill
Jill Carroll
Virginia Charon
Pat Clark
John Corso
Bill Cowan
Chuck Crafts
Mickey Crofford
Dean Cundey

<u>D</u>

Sean Daniel
Michael Day
Robert Destri
George Dickerson
Syd Dutton

<u>E</u>

Gordon Ecker
Bob Ellsworth

<u>F</u>

Ron Filbert
Philip Flad
Richard Franklin
Dennis Franz
Ben Frommer
Gary Frommer

<u>G</u>

Robert Garcia
Lee Garlington
Sue Gauthier
Stan Gilbert
Hugh Gillin
Dennis Glouner
Jerry Goldsmith
David Gonzales
Richard Gonzales
Joel Gotler
Bill Gray
Brad Green
Hilton Green
Pam Green
Marsh Green
Wendy Green
Bill Greenberg
Betty Griffin

<u>H</u>

Ken Hall
Mike Harris
Ben Hartigan
Tracy Heflin
Roger Heman
Chris Hendrie
Tom Holland
Laszlo Horvath

<u>I</u>

<u>J</u>

Greg Jensen
Trace Johnson
Sandra Jones

<u>K</u>

Randy Kelley
Ray Kinzer
Randall Kleiser
Doug Knapp

<u>L</u>

Ray La Porte
Dan Leahy
Lynn Ledgerwood
Cari Lewis
Steve Livingston
Robert Loggia (3)
Michael Lomazow
Andrew London
Max London

<u>M</u>

Tim Maier
Bill Major
Lisa Marmon
Terry Marshall
Thom Marshall
Paul Martia
Barbara Martin
Bill Masten
Les Mayfield
Jo McCarthy
Michael McCracken
Jackie McNamara (3)
Tony Milch
Vera Miles
Tony Monzo
Mike Moramarco
Glenn Morgan
Arthur Morton

<u>N</u>

Terry Nelson
John Nettles
Bob Newlan

<u>O</u>

Brian O'Dowd
Bob O'Neil
Mike Orefice
Don Ortiz
Dan Ostroff

<u>P</u>

Kurt Paul
Berry Perkins
Osgood Perkins
Florence Petersen
Levester Peterson
Tom Piper, Jr.
Tom Piper, Sr.
Rebecca Polack
Jennifer Polito

<u>Q</u>

<u>R</u>

Stephanie Revesz
John Roesch
Joan Rowe
Star Runyan

<u>S</u>

Marla Schlom
Bernard Schwartz
Robert Schwartz
Phil Scott
Kathy Sedolkin
Mark Server
Tanya Sharp
Rex Slinkard
Thaddeus Smith
David Spence (3)
Wylie Stateman
Raymond Stella

<u>T</u>

Stephen Tate
Bill Taylor
Meg Tilly
Robert Traynor

<u>U</u>

<u>V</u>

<u>W</u>

Mark Walthour
Wally Weber
Albert Whitlock
Mark Whitlock
Gene Whittington
Mike Wilhoit
Robert Widin
Mike Wilhoit
Monty Woodard
Ronald Woodward

<u>X/Y</u>

Bob Yannetti
Bob Yerkes

<u>Z</u>

George Zaloom
John Zemansky
Don Zepfel

Press Kit

PSYCHO II

PRESS INFORMATION
From Universal An MCA Company

As of April 8, 1983

UNIVERSAL PICTURES
and
OAK INDUSTRIES
PRESENT

A BERNARD SCHWARTZ PRODUCTION

ANTHONY PERKINS

in

"PSYCHO II"

VERA MILES

ROBERT LOGGIA

and

MEG TILLY

Co-Starring

DENNIS FRANZ

HUGH GILLIN

ROBERT ALAN BROWNE

Produced by   Directed by
HILTON A. GREEN   RICHARD FRANKLIN

Executive Producer   Written by
BERNARD SCHWARTZ   TOM HOLLAND

A UNIVERSAL-OAK PICTURE

(more)

UNIVERSAL
STUDIOS

THE CAST

```
Norman Bates...................................ANTHONY PERKINS
Lila.....................................VERA MILES
Mary.....................................MEG TILLY
Dr. Raymond.................................ROBERT LOGGIA
Toomey......................................DENNIS FRANZ
Sheriff Hunt................................HUGH GILLIN
Mrs. Spool.................................CLAUDIA BRYAR
Statler..................................ROBERT ALAN BROWNE
Judge....................................BEN HARTIGAN
Myrna....................................LEE GARLINGTON
Josh.....................................TIM MAIER
Kim......................................JILL CARROLL
Deputy Pool................................CHRIS HENDRIE
Deputy Norris..............................TOM HOLLAND
D.A......................................MICHAEL LOMAZOW
Public Defender...........................ROBERT DESTRI
Young Norman..............................OSGOOD PERKINS
Sexton...................................BEN FROMMER
Diver....................................GENE WHITTINGTON
Desk Clerk................................ROBERT TRAYNOR
County Sheriff............................GEORGE DICKERSON
Deputy Sheriff...........................THADDEUS SMITH
Deputy Woman..............................SHEILA K. ADAMS
Deputy Clerk..............................VICTORIA BROWN
Stunt Man.................................BOB YERKES
```

THE CREDITS

```
Produced by................................HILTON A. GREEN
Directed by................................RICHARD FRANKLIN
Written by.................................TOM HOLLAND
Executive Producer.........................BERNARD SCHWARTZ
Director of Photography....................DEAN CUNDEY
Production Designer........................JOHN W. CORSO
Edited by..................................ANDREW LONDON
Special Visual Effects by..................ALBERT WHITLOCK
Music by...................................JERRY GOLDSMITH
Unit Production Manager....................BILL GRAY
First Assistant Director...................DON ZEPFEL
Second Assistant Director..................LISA MARMON
Set Decorations............................JENNIFER POLITO
Assistant Art Director.....................JAMES ALLEN
Property Master............................JOHN ZEMANSKY
Assistant Property Master..................ROBERT K. WIDIN
Casting by.................................JACKIE McNAMARA
```

(more)

THE CREDITS (cont'd)

```
Based on Characters Created by..................ROBERT BLOCH
Matte Photography by...........................BILL TAYLOR
...............................................DENNIS GLOUNER
Matte Artist...................................SYD DUTTON
Camera Operator........................RAYMOND STELLA S.O.C.
Assistant Cameramen............................CLYDE E. BRYAN
...............................................STEVE TATE
Script Supervisor......................BETTY ABBOTT GRIFFIN
Assistant Film Editor..........................DAVID SPENCE
Make-Up................................MICHAEL McCRACKEN
...............................................CHUCK CRAFTS
Hair Stylist...................................JO McCARTHY
Men's Costumes.........................ROBERT ELLSWORTH
...............................................BRIAN O'DOWD
Women's Costumes.................. .....MARLA DENISE SCHLOM
Sound Mixer....................................JIM ALEXANDER
Sound Re-Recording.............................ROGER HEMAN
...............................................PHILIP FLAD
...............................................REX SLINKARD
Recordist......................................MARK S. SERVER
Boom Operator..................................PATRICK CLARK
Orchestration..................................ARTHUR MORTON
Music Editor...................................KENNETH HALL
Music Scoring Mixer............................MICKEY CROFFORD
Sound Design by................................ANDREW LONDON
Supervising Sound Editor.................GORDON ECKER, JR.
.......................................(wallaWorks)
ADR Editor.............................STAN GILBERT, M.P.S.E.
Sound Editors..................................LON E. BENDER
...............................................RANDY KELLEY
...............................................ANTHONY R. MILCH
...............................................MIKE WILHOIT
Foley Editor...................................BOB NEWLAN
Assistant Sound Editors........................DONALD ORTIZ
...............................................CARI LEWIS
Foley by.......................................JOHN ROESCH
...............................................JOAN ROWE
Special Effects........................MELBOURNE ARNOLD
Lead Man.......................................ROBERT GARCIA
Craft Service..........................PAUL F. MARTIA
Standby Painter................................RAY LA PORTE
Gaffer.................................MARK D. WALTHOUR
Best Boys......................................THOM MARSHALL
...............................................MICHAEL OREFICE
Electricians...........................TERRY H. MARSHALL, JR.
...............................................MONTY WOODARD
Transportation Captains........................TONY MONZO
...............................................TONY EMERZIAN
Key Grip...............................RONALD T. WOODWARD
```

(more)

THE CREDITS (Cont'd)

```
Dolly Grip.....................................RICHARD BABIN
2nd Grip......................................LASZLO HORVATH
Grips............................................RAY KINSER
.........................................JOHN HENRY NETTLES
Swing Gang...................................BRUCE ANDREWS
Greensman......................................BILL COWAN
Negative Cutter................................WALLY WEBER
DGA Trainee..................................ROBERT YANNETTI
Titles & Optical Effects.....................UNIVERSAL TITLE
Production Secretary............................PAM BREWER
Assistant to Executive Producer................SANDRA JONES
Assistants to Producer........................LES MAYFIELD
...........................................GEORGE ZALOOM
Assistant to Mr. Franklin.....................SETH GECHTER
Unit Publicist...................... ..........JOAN EISENBERG
Stills......................................RON BATZDORFF
```

ORIGINAL SOUNDTRACK ALBUM AVAILABLE ON
MCA RECORDS AND TAPES

PANAFLEX ® CAMERA and LENSES BY PANAVISION ®

COLOR BY TECHNICOLOR ®

Recorded in DOLBY STEREO

THE PRODUCERS WISH TO ACKNOWLEDGE THEIR DEBT TO
SIR ALFRED HITCHCOCK

Running Time: 113 Minutes

MPAA Rating: R

*   *   *

April 8, 1983

"PSYCHO II"

(Production Notes)

The old, gothic Victorian house stands idle and dusty atop a hill. Below, a broken neon sign flashes on, announcing vacancies in a run-down motel.

After 22 years, Norman Bates is back home.

In "Psycho II," the Universal-Oak Pictures' sequel to Alfred Hitchcock's classic 1960 gothic thriller, Norman has spruced up the old Bates Motel in anticipation of new customers. The location is still the same: in the shadow of that in-famous house where young Norman committed some rather heinous crimes 22 years ago. But that's all in the past. Norman has been declared legally restored to sanity by the court and has returned to society, a rehabilitated man.

Room reservations are being taken.

Anthony Perkins stars in "Psycho II," along with Vera Miles, reprising their roles from the original motion picture, with Meg Tilly and Robert Loggia co-starring as new characters. Australian filmmaker Richard Franklin directed his first American film from an original screenplay by Tom Holland. A Bernard Schwartz Production, Hilton Green produced, and Bernard Schwartz served as the executive producer.

UNIVERSAL
STUDIOS

(more)

THE BACKGROUND

The concept for a sequel to "Psycho" began when Universal Pictures and Oak Media Development Corporation entered into a four-film co-production venture in early 1982. Veteran motion picture and television executive Bernard Schwartz would serve as executive producer on the four projects. Of the several project ideas discussed, the title "Psycho II" received the most favorable reaction and was given the green light as the first film to be produced by this partnership.

"The idea of 'Psycho II' appealed to me," says Bernard Schwartz. "It had a tremendous awareness; it was a classic, and it had a theme that interested me (the question of releasing the criminally insane from institutions) which was the basis to trigger a legitimate sequel to 'Psycho.'"

Hilton Green was then chosen as the producer of "Psycho II." His background as Alfred Hitchcock's first assistant director on the original "Psycho" and on the <u>Alfred Hitchcock Presents</u> television series and as the production manager on "Marnie," proved to be an invaluable asset to the making of the sequel.

Both Schwartz and Green agreed that Richard Franklin would be the perfect candidate to direct "Psycho II" because of his expertise in handling thrillers of the Hitchcock genre and his tremendous respect for Hitchcock's works. Completing the team, screenwriter Tom Holland was chosen to write the original script.

(more)

"I think Tom's script is rather unique and will surprise a lot of people," remarks Green. "'Psycho' had its own tremendous twists of plot, so the question remained, 'how do you do it again?' I think we have an excellent story that can rest on its own laurels and doesn't have to lean on its predecessor. When he read the script, Anthony Perkins was convinced that he should reprise the role of Norman Bates. Adding Vera Miles rounded out all the elements we needed for a good start."

One of the most important elements for director Franklin was to capture the same tone and mood of "Psycho." The original was "part horror film, part gothic melodrama and part black comedy all mixed together," comments Franklin. "'Psycho II' continues in the same genre. It is a psychological thriller that works on one level as a fairly complex puzzle to be unraveled, while keeping us emotionally invovled on another level.

"I've tried to remember the 'Psycho' I saw in 1960, when I sneaked into a theatre five times as a 12-year-old. I thought Janet Leigh in her bra was the most decadent adult thing I'd ever seen. Hitchcock was most disapproving of her. She had stepped outside the bounds of the law and what was considered right and became a victim of the forces of chaos, as in Greek tragedy. I think we've taken the same things and worked with them in 'Psycho II.'"

Casting Anthony Perkins as Norman Bates was a key element necessary to the success of "Psycho II." "For years I'd resisted the whole idea of 'Psycho' exposure," comments Perkins. "I felt 'Psycho' had been sufficient in itself. It was a well-

(more)

constructed story. It never occurred to me there would be more
juice in those characters. When I received Tom Holland's
script I liked it very much. It is a well-crafted narrative
which is a logical extension of the first story. It is really
Norman's story.

"I don't think I've ever played anyone quite like him,"
Perkins continues. "Of course, Norman has changed after 22
years in an institution. He's more educated about himself now
and has the knowledge that he has the potential of being dan-
gerous. He is also very trusting and generous of spirit.
He's a likeable guy with some very winning qualities. I think
the audience will feel compassion for him."

Vera Miles shares Perkins' enthusiasm for the project.
She had also seen several other scripts over the years which
she felt did not capture the flavor of the original. "When
I read this one," she says, "I thought it was quite good. For
years movies have been trying not to duplicate 'Psycho,' but
to out-ugly and out-terror it. What is unique about this film
is that it's been kept in the genre of Hitchcock, which is always tasteful. It puts terror in the mind of the audience,
not in the eye of the viewer."

THE PRODUCTION

When Alfred Hitchcock made "Psycho" in 1960, he did it
as an experiment in the sense that he wanted to prove to Hollywood and to himself that he didn't necessarily have to spend

(more)

a lot of money to make a great movie. He used his television crew and shot it on a very low budget and a short schedule in black and white.

Producer Hilton Green felt very strongly that a major studio could make a quality low budget movie today. "I don't like the words 'low budget,' comments Green, "but I think the key to it is no waste; put everything on the screen. If the movie is designed carefully and plotted out, there is no reason, with the cooperation of the director, that you can't achieve quality without a lot of money.

"This particular project leant itself to that because it was a studio picture," he continues. "There weren't a lot of exotic locations; it wasn't a tremendous cast. Basically the house is one of the stars of the piece and we were fortunate to have part of it already here on the lot at Universal."

It was essential to the authenticity of "Psycho II" to use the original house from "Psycho" -- the brooding, Victorian gothic mansion on the hill which has become one of the most famous images in film history. "The house is as important as Norman," says Franklin. "It is a time capsule. It represents all the values of his past, his mother and society. It's 22 years later, but Norman and the house haven't changed very much. They are both time capsules."

When Universal Studios' back lot was redesigned, the "Psycho" house was moved from its original location. Green and Franklin found another site on the lot that best duplicated the original location. Production designer John Corso ("Coal

(more)

Miner's Daughter," "Xanadu") had the hill graded and moved the
house to it's new site, where he aged it 22 years. Using photographs from the original film, Corso reconstructed the Bates
Motel below the house. The steps up to the house were cast
from a mold for the stone pattern and constructed in the proper perspective to the motel below.

The Bates Motel was built from scratch, using photographs
and some old blueprints. Only 40 feet of the front side of
the motel was filmed. The rest of it and the flashing neon
sign were done optically with matte artistry. These special
visual effects were designed by Academy Award-winner Albert
Whitlock, who has dozens of Hitchcock films to his credits.

Set decorator Jennifer Polito was faced with finding props
and set dressings to match those seen in the house and the
motel in the original film. The only clues she had at her
disposal were the film itself and a book of frame-by-frame
stills, both, of course, in black and white. Many times she
had to rely on wall shadows to recreate the items on these
sets. Producer Green helped to verify their accuracy from his
memory of the original sets.

She visited all the rental houses in Los Angeles with her
photographs. Her persistence paid off: she found many of the
original pieces, including two Tiffany lamps, the stuffed owl
and raven, the brass hands seen in "mother's" room, the bedroom fireplace, the old Victorian bed and armoire, and even the
40-foot-long threadbare runner for the stairs.

The new sets, all of which were constructed on stages at
Universal Studios, consist of a courtroom, a sheriff's office,

(more)

a diner, and a hotel bar and lobby.

To achieve the tone and mood that Franklin knew were essential for this psychological thriller, he opted for the German Expressionist cinematic style, a form which had influenced Hitchcock also.

In pre-production Franklin and cinematographer Dean Cundey ("The Thing," "Escape From New York," "Halloween") screened several legendary films which employed the German Expressionist style of exaggerated sets and deep shadow areas. They also went through some of Hitchcock's films, particularly "The Lodger," his 1926 film about Jack the Ripper which is probably the closest film to "Psycho" that he ever made.

"Because 'Psycho' had built up a legend about itself, we had to create a sequel which measures up as much to the legend in terms of look as to the actual film itself," remarks Cundey. "Part of this meant creating the sensation for the audience that they are seeing a continuation of the first film in terms of style and mood. In doing that, Richard went back to the original film quite a bit to find particular shots that will strike a note in the mind of the audience so that they remember the same feeling from a particular scene or a particular shot and then carry it on past that into the new film.

"We referred a lot to frame blow-ups and the original film for the mood and feeling of certain sequences, as well as for set dressings," says Cundey. "To some extent we've duplicated the feeling of some of the sequences, doing the same camera moves in the same sets and moving the actors in the same way."

(more)

Cundey had the opportunity of utilizing a Louma crane,
which is a relatively new technological advance in camera systems,
on a special shot that Franklin wanted. As Cundey describes
it, the Louma crane "has a camera which is mounted on the end
of a boom or pole that can be anywhere from 12 to 24 feet long.
This camera has a TV monitor and is manipulated by the operator
who watches the camera through a TV system. As such, you are
only limited by where you can poke the end of the pole that
has the camera on it."

The Louma crane was used for a high shot outside the "Psycho"
house. It was lifted over 40 feet in the air to shoot through
the little round window at the top of the house and then maneu-
vered all the way down to ground level, in one move, after
creeping along the roof line.

The film was shot in stark, high contrast color to give
it the texture of the original movie's black-and-white look.
Cundey's style of lighting creates areas where danger could be
lurking to elevate the suspense level for the audience. He
used Kodak's new 5293 High Speed Negative film to create high
contrast at low levels of light.

Involving the audience emotionally was a major concern of
Hitchcock, and it is to Richard Franklin also.

"I've used the camera, the soundtrack, the score, and the
performances," he says, "to involve the audience on a psychological roller coaster."

(more)

THE CAST

In "Psycho II" ANTHONY PERKINS stars as Norman Bates, re-creating the role he made famous 22 years ago in the original "Psycho."

Throughout his long acting career Perkins has had the opportunity to display his versatility in hundreds of distinct roles in films, television and the theatre.

While he was attending Rollins College in Florida, in 1953, Perkins travelled to Hollywood to audition for his first movie, "The Actress." He made an impressive film debut working with Jean Simmons and Spencer Tracy.

After the film, he transferred to Columbia University in New York, where he majored in history. He was soon signed by Elia Kazan to portray the young boy in the Broadway production of Tea And Sympathy. At the cost of his college degree, he performed in the play on Broadway and on tour for more than a year.

He was again called to Hollywood to star as Gary Cooper's son in William Wyler's "Friendly Persuasion." His other early films include "Fear Strikes OUt," Eugene O'Neill's "Desire Under The Elms," "Green Mansions," Thornton Wilder's "The Matchmaker," "Tall Story," (co-starring Jane Fonda in her first movie), and "On The Beach."

In 1960, he starred in Alfred Hitchcock's "Psycho" in the role that brought him international attention. The next year he starred with Ingrid Bergman in "Goodbye, Again," for which he won the Cannes International Film Festival best actor award.

(more)

Other films include "Phaedra," "Pretty Poison," "Catch-22," "Play It As It Lays," "Murder On The Orient Express," "The Black Hole," "ffolkes," "Mahagony" and "Remember My Name," (in which he starred with his wife Berry Berenson).

On television he starred in the movie, "Les Miserables," and also appeared with Mary Tyler Moore in the critically acclaimed "First You Cry."

His Broadway appearances have included starring roles in the Frank Loessor musical Greenwillow; Look Homeward Angel; Steambath (which he also directed); Equus, as the doctor, and most recently, Romantic Comedy.

Perkins also collaborated with Stephen Sondheim on the screenplay for the complex mystery film, "The Last Of Sheila."

VERA MILES stars as Lila in "Psycho II," reprising her role from the original motion picture.

While she was in high school Miles entered a beauty contest which led to her appearance in the Miss America Pageant, where she was third runner-up. She took her $2500 prize and her screen contract award and travelled to Hollywood.

Miles considers her ingenue lead in "For Men Only," in 1952, to be her real acting debut. Other films included "The Charge At Feather River," "Tarzan's Hidden Jungle," "Wichita," and "23 Paces To Baker Street."

Concurrently she appeared in scores of live television dramas like Studio One, Hallmark Hall Of Fame, Lux Theatre and Playhouse 90.

                         .(more)

In 1956, she worked with John Ford for the first time in perhaps her favorite film, "The Searchers," co-starring with John Wayne.

Under personal contract to Alfred Hitchcock for six years, Miles starred in "The Wrong Man," with Henry Fonda, and in "Psycho," with Anthony Perkins and Janet Leigh. She did the pilot of the Alfred Hitchcock television series and starred in four television movies for the director, including "Incident At A Corner."

In 1962, she starred in another John Ford film, the classic western, "The Man Who Shot Liberty Valance," with John Wayne and James Stewart. Some of her other films include "Beau James," "The F.B.I. Story," "Follow Me Boys," "Hellfighters" and "The Wild Country."

She has appeared in television series such as Magunum, P.I., Columbo, Mission Impossible, Gunsmoke and many more.

On stage, Miles has starred on tour in 40 Carats, Same Time Next Year, Finishing Touches, The Turn Of The Worm and The Gingerbread Lady.

MEG TILLY portrays the role of Mary in "Psycho II." Tilly was born in California and raised in Victoria, British Columbia. In high school she began dancing and acting in community plays. She and her sister Jenny also sang in the Royal Conservatory Choir, which enabled them to travel and perform in such dis-tinguished places as Westminster Abbey.

After graduation from high school, she moved to New York City to pursue a dancing career. She won a scholarship to

(more)

a dance school and continued until a clumsy partner accidentally dropped her on her back and cut short her dancing ambitions. She gravitated towards acting at this time.

Ironically, her first acting assignment was as a dancer in "Fame," although her few lines wound up on the cutting room floor.

In 1981, she was cast in the role of Jamie Collins, a feisty Oklahoma tomboy in Walt Disney Studios' "Tex." Following this, she appeared in an episode of TV's hit series, Hill Street Blues and an After School Special entitled "The Trouble With Grandpa." She then had the lead in the feature film "One Dark Night."

Tilly is currently in Europe co-starring in the film version of Amadeus, directed by Milos Foreman.

ROBERT LOGGIA co-stars as Dr. Bill Raymond, the psychiatrist who has been treating Norman Bates, in "Psycho II."

His first break in the theatre was a starring role in The Man With The Golden Arm, in 1955, at the Cherry Lane Theatre. On Broadway he then starred in half the run of Lillian Hellman's Toys In The Attic, succeeding Jason Robards. He starred in the Actors Studio production of Three Sisters, and has been a member of that group since 1955.

Off-Broadway Loggia produced and appeared in Passing Through From Exotic Places. He co-starred in Joseph Papp's production of Wedding Band, and in David Rabe's In The Boom Boom Room, the production which heralded the opening of Lincoln Center in New York City.

(more)

His television appearances have included guest starring roles on all the networks and two of his own series: <u>T.H.E. Cat</u> and Walt Disney's <u>The Nine Lives Of Elfego Baca</u>.

On PBS television, Loggia was in the BBC production of "The Chicago Conspiracy Trial" and also in "The Trial Of Inez Garcia." He co-starred with Ingrid Bergman in the television movie, "A Woman Called Golda," portraying Egyptian President Anwar Sadat.

Loggia's feature film credits include "Somebody Up There Likes Me," "Che," "First Love," "The Revenge Of The Pink Panther," "S.O.B.," "Trail Of The Pink Panther," "Curse Of The Pink Panther" and "An Officer And A Gentleman."

As a director Loggia has helmed episodes of <u>Quincy</u>, <u>Magnum, P.I.</u> and <u>Hart To Hart</u>.

<u>THE FILMMAKERS</u>

Director RICHARD FRANKLIN was born in Melbourne, Australia, where he majored in English at Monash University in Melbourne.

His affinity for Alfred Hitchcock films developed when he was 12-years-old and sneaked into a theatre five times to see "Psycho." Because there were no film courses being offered in Australia in the mid-1960s, Franklin transferred to the U.S.C. Film School in 1967.

While at U.S.C. Franklin arranged a three-week retrospective of the films of Alfred Hitchcock and, through this, had his first meeting with his idol, while sharing a stage during a seminar discussion of his films.

(more)

Returning to Australia in 1969, Franklin was an assistant director on a television series called Homicide, and later directed 20 episodes. During this time he also made underground films on weekends.

In 1974, Franklin made his first feature, "The True Story Of Eskimo Nell." This was followed by "Patrick," his multi-award-winning thriller. "Patrick" won awards at film festivals in Sitges, Spain; Avoriaz, France, and the United States, and was selected for screening at the 1979 Los Angeles Filmex.

In 1979, Franklin joined his friend and former U.S.C. classmate, Randal Kleiser, as co-producer of the box-office hit, "The Blue Lagoon." Its success helped him finance his next feature, "Road Games," an Australian-American production starring Stacy Keach and Jamie Lee Curtis.

"Psycho II" is Franklin's American directorial debut.

HILTON GREEN spent 25 years working in various production capacities at MCA/Universal before producing "Psycho II," his first film. During most of that time, Green worked as Alfred Hitchcock's first assistant director on the Alfred Hitchcock Presents television series and as the first assistant director of the original "Psycho" and the production manager of "Marnie."

Green entered the Directors Guild as a second assistant director in 1954. His first job was as the second A.D. of Walt Disney's television series, Davy Crockett. He was then hired as the staff second A.D. of William Wyler's "The Desperate Hours," with Humphrey Bogart.

(more)

After working as a first assistant director on hundreds of television shows in the 1950s, Green began an association with Hitchcock in 1957 which lasted until Hitchcock's death in 1980.

From 1968 to 1979, Green was assistant production manager for Universal's feature production office. He then became vice president and executive in charge of production for the company from 1980 to 1981, when he was assigned to produce "Psycho II."

During those years Green supervised the production of features such as "Airport," "Play Misty For Me," "The Beguiled," "American Graffiti," "Sugarland Express," "The Sting," "Earthquake," "Jaws," "The Hindenburg," "Family Plot," and many more.

TOM HOLLAND wrote the original screenplay of "Psycho II." A native of Highland, New York, Holland began writing when he was in high school. He was also an aspiring actor, and apprenticed in acting and playwriting at the Bucks County Playhouse in Pennsylvania. At the age of 16, he was doing commercials in New York.

After attending Northwestern University Film School in Evanston, Illinois, for a year, he returned to New York in 1964 to pursue his acting career. He quickly landed the lead role in the soap opera, A Time For Us. During the next few years Holland commuted between New York and Hollywood working in television shows such as Chrysler Theatre, The Young Lawyers, Medical Center and Mod Squad.

In 1970, Holland quit acting and entered UCLA as a political science major, graduating Phi Beta Kappa with a BA degree.

(more)

He then went on to UCLA Law School and received a law degree, passing the California bar exam in 1975.

While completing law school Holland returned to writing and wrote his first full script, "The View From 30," with his friend, screenwriter Henry Farrell. From then on, he continued writing and had his third script, "Trixie," optioned by producer Dick Berg.

In 1979, Berg hired Holland to write his first television move "Sweetheart Of Sigma Chi," for ABC. He has since had several screenplays optioned. His films, "The Beast Within" and "Class of '84," starring Perry King and Roddy McDowell, were released in 1982.

Executive producer BERNARD SCHWARTZ was instrumental in bringing together Universal and Oak Media Development Corporation for the four-film co-production venture, with "Psycho II" as the first project.

Schwartz was brought to Hollywood to watch over Howard Hughes's movie interests. He teamed with show business attorney Gregson Bautzer to package movie deals for many of Hollywood's best-known personalities.

One of his duties was to recut a number of silent screen star Buster Keaton's greatest movies into documentary anthologies titled "The Golden Age Of Comedy," "When Comedy Was King," "Days Of Thrills And Laughter," and more. He made the popular television series One Step Beyond followed by The Wackiest Ship In The Army and the "Miss Teen International" TV specials.

(more)

As president of Joseph M. Schenck Enterprises he presided over the production of several successful feature films, including "Journey To The Center Of The Earth," "Eye Of The Cat," "Cold Wind In August," "The Shuttered Room" and "Trackdown."

In 1980, Schwartz produced his first feature, "Coal Miner's Daughter," starring Sissy Spacek. The film received seven Academy Award nominations, the best actress Oscar for Sissy Spacek and the Golden Globe award for best picture.

Schwartz served as the executive producer of "Road Games," which was directed by Richard Franklin.

Cinematographer DEAN CUNDEY is a native of Los Angeles. He attended California State College, Los Angeles, where he studied architecture and graphic design, with intentions of a career as an art director in film. He went to UCLA Film School, where he switched his major to cinematography and studied with James Wong Howe.

Cundey worked at a variety of film jobs gaining experience in the business before he shot his first film, "Brother On The Run." This was followed by "Where The Red Fern Grows," starring James Whitmore; "Rock 'N' Roll High School;" "Roller Boogie" and several others.

He then photographed six thrillers for director John Carpenter: "Halloween," "The Fog," "Escape From New York" and "The Thing." He was also cinematographer on "Halloween II" and "Halloween III."

*   *   *

International Posters

A selection of posters and home media covers from around the world

PSYCHO II
サイコ2

PSYCHO II
ヒッチコック・スリラーの金字塔「サイコ」の続編ここに誕生
サイコ2

ANTHONY PERKINS EN
PSICOSIS II
EL REGRESO DE NORMAN

ANTHONY PERKINS IN
PSYCHO II
15
IT'S 22 YEARS LATER.
AND NORMAN BATES
IS COMING HOME
VERA MILES   MEG TILLY   ROBERT LOGGIA   "PSYCHO II"   TOM HOLLAND   JERRY GOLDSMITH   ALBERT WHITLOCK   DEAN CUNDEY   BERNARD SCHWARTZ   HILTON A. GREEN   RICHARD FRANKLIN   A BERNARD SCHWARTZ PRODUCTION
DOLBY STEREO   SOUNDTRACK AVAILABLE ON MCA RECORDS & TAPES.   A UNIVERSAL-OAK PICTURE. DISTRIBUTED BY UIP.   ©1983 Universal City Studios, Inc./Oak Industries. © UIP 1983

PSYCHO II

Hitchcock was once asked about
the tremendous effect *Psycho* seemed to
have on audiences. He replied,
"You know, I once had a letter from a man
who said, 'My daughter saw the
French film *Diabolique* — that's where the
man rises out of the tub — and he
said 'we can't get her to take a bath any
more and now that she's
seen *Psycho* she won't take a shower,
and she's been very, very difficult
to be around. What should
I do?' I said, 'Dear Sir, send her to
the drycleaner.'"

Published by Marquee Communications Incorporated/Art Direction: Gordon Sibley/Printed in Canada/©1983 University City Studios, Inc.
ALL RIGHTS RESERVED

เขาไม่คิดฆ่า
เขาไม่อยากฆ่า
แต่คนทำให้เขาบ้า
เขาก็เลยต้องฆ่า
ริชาร์ด แฟรงกลิน
กำกับการแสดง
แอนโทนี เพอร์กินส์
วีรา ไมลส์ เม้ก ทิลลี่
โรเบิร์ต โลเกีย
ไซโค 2
PSYCHO II

ANTHONY PERKINS in
PSYCHO II

IT'S 22 YEARS LATER,
AND NORMAN BATES
IS COMING HOME.

VERA MILES   MEG TILLY   ROBERT LOGGIA   "PSYCHO II"   Written By TOM HOLLAND   Music By JERRY GOLDSMITH   Special Visual Effects By ALBERT WHITLOCK

Director of Photography DEAN CUNDEY   Executive Producer BERNARD SCHWARTZ   Produced By HILTON A. GREEN   Directed By RICHARD FRANKLIN   A BERNARD SCHWARTZ PRODUCTION

DOLBY STEREO
IN SELECTED THEATRES

Soundtrack available on MCA Records and Cassettes
© 1982 Universal City Studios, Inc./Oak Industries
A UNIVERSAL RELEASE PICTURE

R RESTRICTED
UNDER 17 REQUIRES ACCOMPANYING
PARENT OR ADULT GUARDIAN

PSYCHO II
ARROW
VIDEO

DIGITAL LASERDISC
PSYCHO II
It's 22 years later,
and Norman Bates
is coming home.
ANTHONY PERKINS in
PSYCHO II
VERA MILES MEG TILLY ROBERT LOGGIA "PSYCHO II"
TOM HOLLAND JERRY GOLDSMITH
ALBERT WHITLOCK DEAN CUNDEY BERNARD SCHWARTZ
HILTON A. GREEN RICHARD FRANKLIN A BERNARD SCHWARTZ Production
digital SOUND STEREO
MCA UNIVERSAL HOME VIDEO
LASER VIDEODISC
PSYCHO II
ANTHONY PERKINS in
PSYCHO II
IT'S 22 YEARS LATER,
AND NORMAN BATES
IS COMING HOME.
STEREO
MCA HOME VIDEO

ANTHONY PERKINS IN
PSYCHO II
IT'S 22 YEARS LATER,
AND NORMAN BATES
IS COMING HOME.

VERA MILES   MEG TILLY   ROBERT LOGGIA   "PSYCHO II"   Written by TOM HOLLAND   Music by JERRY GOLDSMITH   Special Visual Effects by ALBERT WHITLOCK
Director of Photography DEAN CUNDEY   Executive Producer BERNARD SCHWARTZ   Produced by HILTON A. GREEN   Directed by RICHARD FRANKLIN   A BERNARD SCHWARTZ PRODUCTION

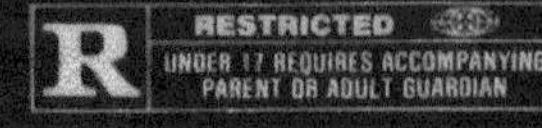

DOLBY STEREO
IN SELECTED THEATRES
Soundtrack available on MCA Records and Cassettes
© 1982 Universal City Studios, Inc./Oak Industries
A UNIVERSAL RELEASE
R RESTRICTED
UNDER 17 REQUIRES ACCOMPANYING
PARENT OR ADULT GUARDIAN

STARTS JUNE 3RD AT SELECTED THEATRES

ANTHONY PERKINS i
PSYCHO II
DET ÄR 22 ÅR SENARE,
OCH NORMAN BATES HAR
KOMMIT HEM IGEN...
VERA MILES   MEG TILLY   ROBERT LOGGIA   "PSYCHO II"   Written By TOM HOLLAND   Music By JERRY GOLDSMITH   Special Visual Effects by ALBERT WHITLOCK
Director of Photography DEAN CUNDEY   Executive Producer BERNARD SCHWARTZ   Produced By HILTON A. GREEN   Directed By RICHARD FRANKLIN   A BERNARD SCHWARTZ PRODUCTION
DOLBY STEREO
IN SELECTED THEATRES
Musiken ur filmen finns på skiva och kassett från polygram
© 1982 Universal City Studios, Inc. / Oak Industries
UIP FÄRG

ANTHONY PERKINS IN
PSYCHO II
IT'S 22 YEARS LATER,
AND NORMAN BATES
IS COMING HOME.
VERA MILES MEG TILLY ROBERT LOGGIA "PSYCHO II" Written By TOM HOLLAND Music By JERRY GOLDSMITH Special Visual Effects By ALBERT WHITLOCK
Director of Photography DEAN CUNDEY Executive Producer BERNARD SCHWARTZ Produced By HILTON A. GREEN Directed By RICHARD FRANKLIN A BERNARD SCHWARTZ PRODUCTION
A UNIVERSAL OAK PICTURE
R RESTRICTED UNDER 17 REQUIRES ACCOMPANYING PARENT OR ADULT GUARDIAN
COMING SOON TO SELECTED THEATRES

CIC
VIDEO

22 VUOTTA ON KULUNUT
JA NORMAN BATES PALAA KOTIIN ...
ANTHONY PERKINS
PSYKO II
PSYKO II
MEG TILLY VERA MILES ROBERT LOGGIA 'PSYCHO II' Written By TOM HOLLAND Music By JERRY GOLDSMITH
Special Visual Effects By ALBERT WHITLOCK Director of Photography DEAN CUNDEY Executive Producer BERNARD SCHWARTZ
Produced By HILTON A. GREEN Directed By RICHARD FRANKLIN A BERNARD SCHWARTZ PRODUCTION

ESSELTE VIDEO

22 ans après, Norman Bates rentre chez lui.
ANTHONY PERKINS DANS
PSYCHOSE 2
VERA MILES   MEG TILLY   ROBERT LOGGIA   "PSYCHOSE II"   Écrit par TOM HOLLAND   Musique de JERRY GOLDSMITH   Effets Spéciaux Visuels ALBERT WHITLOCK
Directeur de la Photographie DEAN CUNDEY   Producteur Exécutif BERNARD SCHWARTZ   Produit par HILTON A. GREEN   Réalisé par RICHARD FRANKLIN   UNE PRODUCTION BERNARD SCHWARTZ
DOLBY STEREO
DANS CERTAINES SALLES
1982 Universal City Studios Inc. / Oak Industries
UN FILM UNIVERSAL DISTRIBUÉ PAR CINEMA INTERNATIONAL CORPORATION

PSYCHO II
ARROW VIDEO
18

ANTHONY PERKINS IN
PSYCHO II
ES IST 22 JAHRE SPÄTER. UND NORMAN BATES KOMMT NACH HAUSE.

ANTHONY PERKINS in
PSYCHO II
ES IST 22 JAHRE SPÄTER
UND NORMAN BATES
KOMMT NACH HAUSE.
VERA MILES · MEG TILLY · ROBERT LOGGIA "PSYCHO II" TOM HOLLAND JERRY GOLDSMITH ALBERT WHITLOCK
DEAN CUNDEY BERNARD SCHWARTZ HILTON A. GREEN RICHARD FRANKLIN BERNARD SCHWARTZ

ANTHONY PERKINS en
PSICOSIS
2ª PARTE
(El regreso de Norman)
22 años después
Norman Bates
vuelve a casa.
VERA MILES · MEG TILLY · ROBERT LOGGIA · "PSYCHO II" · Escrita por TOM HOLLAND
Música por JERRY GOLDSMITH · Efectos visuales especiales por ALBERT WHITLOCK
Director de fotografía DEAN CUNDEY · Productor Ejecutivo BERNARD SCHWARTZ
Producida por HILTON A. GREEN · Dirigida por RICHARD FRANKLIN · Una producción de BERNARD SCHWARTZ
UNA PELICULA UNIVERSAL-OAK
DISTRIBUIDA POR CINEMA INTERNATIONAL CORPORATION

PSYCHO II

ANTHONY PERKINS IN
PSYCHO II

ANTHONY PERKINS IN
PSYCHO II
IT'S 22 YEARS LATER,
AND NORMAN BATES
IS COMING HOME.

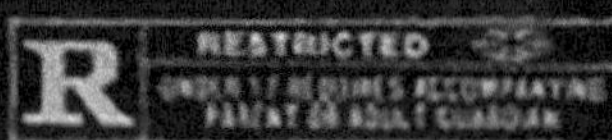

ANTHONY PERKINS IN
PSYCHO II
IT'S 22 YEARS LATER,
AND NORMAN BATES
IS COMING HOME
DOLBY STEREO
Soundtrack available on MCA Records and Cassettes
RESTRICTED
UNDER 17 REQUIRES ACCOMPANYING
PARENT OR ADULT GUARDIAN
R

NEUES
Film-PROGRAMM
Nr. 7958
PSYCHO II

PSYCHO II

ANTHONY PERKINS in

PSYCHO II

Color/1 Hr. 53 Mins./R

In 1960, Alfred Hitchcock shocked audiences around the world and made screen history with his Gothic horror masterpiece, *Psycho*. Now, 22 years later, the Bates Motel is back in business and screams of terror are once again being heard as the long-awaited sequel, *Psycho II*, comes to the screen. Anthony Perkins, who starred as Norman Bates, and Vera Miles, who played the sister of the shower murder victim, recreate their memorable roles from the original. In addition, movie buffs will be heartened to know that the producer of the film was Hitchcock's first assistant director in *Psycho*, and the director is a serious Hitchcock scholar. The result is a movie that the New York Daily News has called, "a winner", and KABC-TV describes as "even more intense than the original".

ANTHONY PERKINS in *PSYCHO II* • VERA MILES • MEG TILLY • ROBERT LOGGIA • *PSYCHO II* • Written by TOM HOLLAND • Music by JERRY GOLDSMITH • Special Visual Effects by ALBERT WHITLOCK • Director of Photography DEAN CUNDEY • Executive Producer BERNARD SCHWARTZ • Produced by HILTON A. GREEN • Directed by RICHARD FRANKLIN • A BERNARD SCHWARTZ Production • A UNIVERSAL OAK PICTURE. • ©1983 Universal City Studios, Inc, and Oak Industries. All Rights Reserved.

This Videocassette has been recorded in stereo with Dolby "B" type noise reduction and is compatible for monaural playback with all VHS equipment.
During playback set Dolby "B" N.R. switch to the on position.
Warning: The motion picture contained in this videocassette is protected under the copyright laws of the United States and other countries. This cassette is sold for home use only and all other rights are expressly reserved by the copyright owner of such motion picture. Any copying or public performance of such motion picture is strictly prohibited and may subject the offender to civil liability and severe criminal penalties (Title 17, United States Code, Sections 501 and 506).

MCA HOME VIDEO

70 UNIVERSAL CITY PLAZA, UNIVERSAL CITY, CA 91608
Dolby and the double D symbol are trademarks of Dolby Laboratories Licensing Corporation.

MCA HOME VIDEO

© 1983 MCA Home Video, Inc. All rights reserved. Printed in USA

ANTHONY PERKINS in

PSYCHO II

STEREO
DOLBY SYSTEM

VHS
VHS 80008

MCA HOME VIDEO

STEREO

Swedish edition

UNIVERSAL

PSYCHO II

I den här skrämmande uppföljaren till Alfred Hitchcocks berömda rysare kommer den galne Norman Bates hem till det gamla huset efter 22 år på mentalsjukhus. Nedanför huset ligger fortfarande det slitna motellet, där Janet Leigh blev mördad i den klassiska duschscenen. När Norman går in i huset, är allt som förr. Hans mor ropar på honom och ger order om ett nytt mord. Problemet är att modern varit död i 22 år!

ANTHONY PERKINS in *PSYCHO II* • VERA MILES • MEG TILLY • ROBERT LOGGIA • Written by TOM HOLLAND • Music by JERRY GOLDSMITH • Special Visual Effects by ALBERT WHITLOCK • Director of Photography DEAN CUNDEY • Executive Producer BERNARD SCHWARTZ • Produced by HILTON A. GREEN • Directed by RICHARD FRANKLIN • A BERNARD SCHWARTZ Production • A UNIVERSAL OAK PICTURE. ©1983 Universal City Studios, Inc. and Oak Industries. All Rights Reserved.

PSYCHO II		
Rysare	Speltid 1 tim 48 min	Tillåten fr. 15 år
Inspelad 1983	Färg	Svensk text

Hi-Fi

UNIVERSAL

Denna Universal film distribueras i Sverige av Universal Pictures (Nordic) AB
Ansvarig utgivare: Damen Kinemsley-Hill

Varning! Denna videokassetts programinnehåll är skydd enligt upphovsrättslagen. Innehavaren av rättigheterna till detta program är Universal Pictures (Nordic) AB. Videokassetten får endast köphandtabilitas släpt behörigheten genom försäljning. Kassetten får icke hyllas visas offentligt, i slutna sällskap eller i kabelnät. All kopiering, även sådan för privat bruk, är förbjuden. **Otillåten användning medför ersättningsskyldighet, samt kan också medföra andra rättsliga konsekvenser, och även åtal.**
Ansvarig utgivare: Damen Kinemsley-Hill

0 044004 480635

© 1989 Universal Studios. All Rights Reserved

SS0448063

RUNNING TIME APPROX.
108 Mins. COLOUR
PSYCHO II
It's 22 Years Later,
and Norman Bates
is coming home.
In 1960, Alfred Hitchcock shocked audiences around the world and made screen history with his Gothic horror masterpiece, Psycho. Now, 22 years later, the Bates Motel is back in business and screams of terror are once again being heard as the long-awaited sequel, Psycho II, comes to the screen. Anthony Perkins, who starred as Norman Bates, and Vera Miles, who played the sister of the shower murder victim, recreate their memorable roles from the original. In addition, movie buffs will be heartened to know that the producer of the film was Hitchcock's first assistant director in Psycho, and the director is a serious Hitchcock scholar. The result is a movie that the New York Daily News has called, "a winner."
Starring
ANTHONY PERKINS
PSYCHO II
A
45
BETA PAL
BEA 1090
CIC VIDEO
CIC VIDEO

PSYCHO II
CIC VIDEO
PSYCHO II
PSYCHO II
In 1960, Alfred Hitchcock shocked audiences around the world and made screen history with his Gothic horror masterpiece, Psycho. Now, 22 years later, the Bates Motel is back in business and screams of terror are once again being heard as the long-awaited sequel, Psycho II, comes to the screen. Anthony Perkins, who starred as Norman Bates, and Vera Miles, who played the sister of the shower murder victim, recreate their memorable roles from the original. In addition, movie buffs will be heartened to know that the producer of the film was Hitchcock's first assistant director in Psycho, and the director is a serious Hitchcock scholar. The result is a movie that the New York Daily News has called, "a winner."
© 1982 UNIVERSAL CITY STUDIOS INC AND OAK INDUSTRIES. ALL RIGHTS RESERVED.
Running Time Approx. 108 minutes   Colour
UWAGA: Wszelkie prawa do tej kasety włączone z głosem nagranym na kasecie zastrzeżone.
It's 22 Years Later,
and Norman Bates
is coming home.
CIC VIDEO

www.ingramcontent.com/pod-product-compliance
Lightning Source LLC
Chambersburg PA
CBHW041730100726
47973CB00010B/164